U.S. Trade Strategy
Free Versus Fair

By Daniel W. Drezner

Critical Policy Choices

COUNCIL ON FOREIGN RELATIONS

Sponsored by the Maurice R. Greenberg Center
for Geoeconomic Studies

Founded in 1921, the Council on Foreign Relations is an independent, national member-ship organization and a nonpartisan center for scholars dedicated to producing and dis-seminating ideas so that individual and corporate members, as well as policymakers, journalists, students, and interested citizens in the United States and other countries, can better understand the world and the foreign policy choices facing the United States and other governments. The Council does this by convening meetings; conducting a wide-rang-ing Studies Program; publishing *Foreign Affairs*, the preeminent journal covering inter-national affairs and U.S. foreign policy; maintaining a diverse membership; sponsoring Independent Task Forces; and providing up-to-date information about the world and U.S. foreign policy on the Council's website, www.cfr.org.

THE COUNCIL TAKES NO INSTITUTIONAL POSITION ON POLICY ISSUES AND HAS NO AFFILIATION WITH THE U.S. GOVERNMENT. ALL STATE-MENTS OF FACT AND EXPRESSIONS OF OPINION CONTAINED IN ITS PUB-LICATIONS ARE THE SOLE RESPONSIBILITY OF THE AUTHOR OR AUTHORS.

This is the seventh volume in the "Critical Policy Choices" series (formerly known as "Coun-cil Policy Initiatives") sponsored and published by the Council on Foreign Relations. The series is designed to encourage informed debate of important foreign policy issues by pre-senting well-developed arguments for each of the principal competing policy approaches in a format that is intended for use by professors, students, and the interested public. This volume benefited from the comments of a number of distinguished experts, but responsi-bility for the final text remains with the author.

Critical Policy Choices are distributed by the Brookings Institution Press (1-800-275-1447). For further information about the Council or this book, please write to the Coun-cil on Foreign Relations, 58 East 68th Street, New York, NY 10021, or call the Communications office at 212-434-9400. Visit the Council's website at www.cfr.org.

CONTENTS

FOREWORD

Trade now accounts for nearly a quarter of America's gross domestic product, double what it was twenty-five years ago. Trade lies at the intersection of two prominent concerns facing America: its economy and its foreign policy. Increasingly, foreign economic policy is also being interwoven into a variety of other important concerns such as national security, employment stability, environmental protection, labor standards, globalization, health issues, immigration, and monetary policy. Today, trade policy affects more decisions and more issues on the U.S. agenda and will have a greater impact on Americans and foreigners than ever before.

A rough consensus exists among policymakers that promoting trade expansion throughout the world serves the national interests of the United States. Experts disagree, however, on how best to accomplish that goal. Daniel Drezner's Critical Policy Choices (CPC) volume suggests two alternative means through which to pursue this goal. The "free trade" approach seeks to ensure the full realization of the economic and political benefits of free trade. It recommends a renewed commitment to the success of the Doha round of trade negotiations through top-level U.S. involvement in the negotiations and a willingness to resist protectionist pressures regarding issues such as outsourcing, textiles, and agriculture. The "fair trade" approach seeks to balance the economic benefits of free trade with other values—community stability and income security, for instance—that may be compromised by an aggressive free trade policy. The approach recommends a tougher stance, in trade negotiations and in Congress, to ensure receptivity to American exports and to stem the tide of outsourcing and other potential threats to U.S. interests.

Beyond the question of whether trade should be free or fair, policymakers must cope with four recurring challenges. The first challenge is managing the current account deficit, which is growing to unprecedented levels. It may be true that trade policy has only a marginal effect on the actual balance of trade, but nevertheless, politics inextricably links the magnitude of the current account deficit to the U.S. ability to expand trade opportunities. Although interest rates and inflation have remained relatively stable, no president can afford to ignore the effects of the trade deficit, or the risk it may pose to the U.S. economy.

The second challenge covers the intersection of trade policy and a diverse array of other policy issues that traditionally have fallen under different areas of expertise. The accelerating pace of technological innovation and economic globalization are blurring the boundaries between domestic and international regulatory concerns, thrusting formerly domestic issues such as labor standards, intellectual property rights, immigration controls, and environmental protections into the international arena.

The third challenge is a crucial domestic issue that has a profound effect on the political discourse surrounding trade: the distribution of the benefits and burdens of trade expansion. Even though freer trade may benefit the U.S. economy overall, particular individuals will suffer disproportionately as a result of the economic changes caused by trade expansion. The controversy over offshore outsourcing illustrates the potency of these concerns in energizing the public, often against trade liberalization. Meanwhile, some Americans are indeed losing their jobs. The Trade Adjustment Assistance programs are intended to compensate workers for these losses and to help prepare them for jobs in other sectors. To achieve the gains from trade for all Americans, the administration must consider how best to support the relatively few Americans who bear the brunt of trade expansion's harmful repercussions.

The fourth challenge is for the administration to find the right balance among multilateral, regional, bilateral, and unilateral tracks of trade diplomacy. It is certainly possible for these different tracks of trade negotiations to complement one another, but that is not always the case. Each negotiation track has strengths and weaknesses, which depend in part on how the United States wishes to balance the economic, political, and social ends desired from trade expansion.

Because these questions and interlocking policy debates are so complex, and because they engender such strong differences of opinion among respected experts and practitioners, the Council decided to address U.S. trade policy by sponsoring a volume in its CPC series, rather than contrive an artificial consensus on this crucial issue.

Our goal with this CPC is to present clearly and comprehensively the many issues involved in U.S. trade policy and the range of options available to policymakers. We aim to draw attention to this important issue and to inform the public on the range of alternatives; we intend to galvanize serious debate rather than to advocate any particular approach. We use the conceit of a "memo to the president" because this is the most creative way to present the issues from the perspective of the decision-maker, encompassing the many different competing claims on a president's attention. We are mindful that this issue cannot be neatly compressed into just two options, and thus we have endeavored to explain the nuances of the trade debate in four white papers that explore the relevant challenges and policy options in greater detail.

With Doha at a standstill and time running out for the president's congressionally granted trade-promotion authority, it is critical that we take stock of the U.S. position in the global economy, its standing in international institutions such as the World Trade Organization, and the numerous free trade agreements under negotiation; that we contemplate the potential objectives of America's trade agenda, which range from aggressive pursuit of a free trade environment to a moderate approach that prepares the way for future expansion while balancing trade interests against other values; that we consider strategic alternatives to help the United States meet its full range of political and economic goals; and that we weigh the costs and benefits of each approach. The U.S. trade agenda faces formidable challenges today, but it also presents valuable opportunities. This CPC offers insight into both.

I thank Daniel W. Drezner for directing and authoring this install-ment in the CPC series. He has produced a balanced, comprehensive, and educational book, one that translates the complex, often con-fusing connections and linkages of trade policy and the demand-ing discipline of economics into accessible yet sophisticated language. I am also particularly grateful to the advisory commit-tee that helped Professor Drezner strike the appropriate balance while ensuring that the final product reflects the full range of respon-sible opinion.

Richard N. Haass
President
Council on Foreign Relations
June 2006

ACKNOWLEDGMENTS

It is not easy writing a memo to the president, even when the commander in chief is strictly notional. First and foremost, I am grateful to Council President Richard N. Haass and Director of Studies James M. Lindsay for asking me to write this installment of the Council's Critical Policy Choices (CPC) series, which was produced by the Maurice R. Greenberg Center for Geoeconomic Studies. They lent their counsel and confidence to me during the drafting of this document, and I could not have finished it without them. As the acting director of the Maurice R. Greenberg Center for Geoeconomic Studies, Benn Steil offered his valuable insight throughout the first part of the drafting process and helped me stay focused on the big picture; Douglas Holtz-Eakin provided valuable comments once he took up the directorship. The Council generously seconded Joshua Marcuse and James Bergman to help with research and logistics. By handling all of the small stuff, they let me focus almost entirely on the content. The many Washington, DC, research interns for the Council—specifically Lillian Haney, Sean Kimball, Kimberly Lehn, and Nathan Puffer—helped to track down most of the precise data behind the charts and figures. I also thank Patricia Dorff and her colleagues in the Publications Department for shepherding this project through to completion. Traci Nagle did a stellar job of converting some of my jargon-filled paragraphs into accessible prose.

During the drafting of this CPC, two off-the-record meetings were held with an advisory committee of eminent persons in trade policy: Anne L. Alonzo, James L. Bacchus, David A. Baldwin, Steve Charnovitz, Kenneth W. Dam, Stuart E. Eizenstat, Daniel C. Esty, Carla A. Hills, Gary C. Hufbauer, Merit E. Janow, Matthew P. Lantz, Theodore Roosevelt IV, Bruce Stokes, Marina v.N. Whitman, and Charles Wolf Jr. The first meeting was held in Washington, DC (chaired by Lee Feinstein), and the second was held a month later in New York (chaired by David Baldwin). I am exceedingly grateful to the participants of both of those meetings; the conversations around the table were of an exceptionally high caliber. Their input vastly improved this monograph while helping me avoid numerous conceptual and factual minefields. I am particularly grateful to the chairs for ensuring that these meetings proceeded smoothly and fruitfully. In addition, a session was held in Chicago with Council members (chaired by Michael H. Moskow), and I am grateful to all of those participants for their learned feedback—and to the indefatigable Irina A. Faskianos for organizing the event. I wrote most of this while at the University of Chicago; my colleagues there, especially Jacob T. Levy and Shelley Clark, helped clarify my thinking on several development issues. David Victor, Howard Rosen, and Minxin Pei also provided useful advice at critical junctures. As a blogger, I also benefited from the ever-increasing number of sharp blogs on questions of international economics—thank you to Tyler Cowen, J. Bradford DeLong, Arnold Kling, Virginia Postrel, John Quiggin, Brad Setser, and Alex Tabarrok. I gained a great deal of insight into U.S. trade policy because I was able to attend the 2005 Hong Kong Ministerial Conference of the World Trade Organization. I thank Craig Kennedy and the trade and development staff at the German Marshall Fund of the United States for making that possible.

It would have been impossible to write this CPC while also teaching without the assistance and understanding of my students during the 2005 winter quarter—even though they never knew I was writing this book. I am indebted to my teaching assistants, Michelle Lelievre and Nusrat Chowdhury, for helping me appear to be a better and more organized teacher to the undergraduates. I am even more indebted to my family—Erika, Lauren, Sam, and Chester—for providing me with the support and patience necessary to complete this project.

Ordinarily, this is the point in the acknowledgments when the author says the views expressed in the ensuing pages are his and his alone. For this project, that is true and yet not true. It is true that no one else bears responsibility for any errors or omissions in this monograph. It is also true, however, that I disagree with many of the views expressed herein. The nature of a CPC is to present a broad array of policy options and orientations to discuss the issue at hand. At times, this required me to forcefully articulate positions that I would vehemently oppose under most circumstances. In principle, a scholar should be able to understand and defend intellectual positions that are opposed to his own. It was thoroughly enjoyable to put this principle to practical use.

Daniel W. Drezner
June 2006

ACRONYMS AND ABBREVIATIONS

AGOA	African Growth and Opportunity Act
ANWR	Arctic National Wildlife Refuge
APEC	Asia-Pacific Economic Cooperation
ARV	antiretroviral
ASEAN	Association of Southeast Asian Nations
ATAA	Alternative Trade Adjustment Assistance
BLS	Bureau of Labor Statistics
CAFTA	Central American Free Trade Agreement
CNOOC	Chinese National Offshore Oil Corporation
CUSTA	Canada-U.S. Free Trade Agreement
DOE	Department of Energy
DOT	Department of Transportation
EU	European Union
FAA	Federal Aviation Administration
FAO	Food and Agriculture Organization
FTA	free trade agreement
FTAA	Free Trade Area of the Americas
G7	Group of Seven advanced industrialized countries
G20	Group of Twenty advanced developing countries
GAO	Government Accountability Office
GATS	General Agreement on Trade in Services
GATT	General Agreement on Tariffs and Trade
GDP	gross domestic product
GM	genetically modified
GMFUS	German Marshall Fund of the United States
GSP	Generalized System of Preferences
IEEPA	International Emergency Economic Powers Act
IF	Integrated Framework for Trade-Related Technical Assistance
IIE	Institute for International Economics
ILO	International Labor Organization

IMF	International Monetary Fund
IPR	intellectual property rights
MEFTA	Middle Eastern Free Trade Area
MFN	most-favored-nation
NAFTA	North American Free Trade Agreement
NAM	National Association of Manufacturers
NGO	nongovernmental organization
NSS	National Security Strategy
OECD	Organization for Economic Cooperation and Development
OPEC	Organization of Petroleum Exporting Countries
PIPA	Program on International Policy Attitudes
PRI	Institutional Revolutionary Party (Mexico)
R&D	research and development
RII	Regulatory Impediments Initiative
SARS	severe acute respiratory syndrome
SII	Structural Impediments Initiative
SPS	Sanitary and Phytosanitary
STDF	Standards and Trade Development Facility
TAA	Trade Adjustment Assistance
TABD	Transatlantic Business Dialogue
TBT	Technical Barriers to Trade
TPA	Trade Promotion Authority
TRIPS	Trade-Related Aspects of Intellectual Property Rights
TSD	Transatlantic Social Dialogue
UNCTAD	United Nations Conference on Trade and Development
UNDP	United Nations Development Programme
USTR	U.S. Trade Representative
VERs	voluntary export restraints
WHO	World Health Organization
WTO	World Trade Organization

MEMORANDUM TO THE PRESIDENT

From: Assistant to the President for Economic Policy and
            Director of the National Economic Council
Subject: Bottom-up Trade Policy Review

Executive Summary

Trade benefits the United States in many ways. Imports keep prices low and increase the variety of goods available for American consumers. Exports provide high-paying jobs for American workers and higher profits for American firms. Trade improves labor productivity and boosts economic growth. Economic openness helps the United States indirectly advance a number of foreign policy goals: democratization, human rights, the rule of law, and global development. At the same time, freer trade is blamed for job losses, rising inequality, and career insecurity among working-class Americans.

Because of trade's importance to the United States, you recently ordered a bottom-up interagency review of American trade policies. The review concludes that the political landscape of trade policy has shifted dramatically in the past decade. While trade has always intersected with other economic issues, its impact has become so encompassing as to affect the war on terror, environmental regulation, immigration reform, monetary policy, health care, and the welfare state. No president can craft positions on trade issues in a policy vacuum. At the same time, shifts in domestic attitudes and world politics have combined to create one of the least hospitable environments for trade liberalization in recent memory.

Navigating these political waters will require firm leadership on your part. As a first step, you need to articulate your orientation of how the United States should approach trade policy. The advantage of thinking about trade policy in terms of orientation is that it communicates a clear signal to other countries about U.S. preferences. This decision dictates choices about your administration's most pressing trade policy concerns: reviving the moribund Doha round of World Trade Organization (WTO) talks and smoothing the frictions in our bilateral economic relationship with the People's Republic of China.

Simply put, you need to choose between a *free trade or fair trade* orientation for the future. A free trade orientation believes that trade expansion creates significant benefits for American consumers, the American economy, and American foreign policy, while at the same time offers growth opportunities for the rest of the world. The goal of this orientation, therefore, is to reduce as many barriers to U.S. exports and imports as quickly as possible. The first-best method of accomplishing this goal is through an ambitious multilateral trade agenda conducted through the World Trade Organization. The second-best option is to continue pursuing free trade agreements with important trading partners, such as Japan, India, South Korea, and the European Union (EU).

A fair trade orientation assumes that further trade expansion will benefit most Americans only under very specific circumstances. Fair traders believe that unchecked trade expansion increases job insecurity for workers in import-competing sectors and encourages the importation of goods made in ways that violate American standards of labor and environmental policy. The goal of this orientation, therefore, is to regulate the growth of trade so as to minimize social costs—even if it slows the growth of trade and the economic benefits that come with it. That means taking no steps to revive the Doha round without first securing greater access for our exporters, vigorous enforcement of trade rules through multilateral and unilateral measures, and a slowdown in bilateral free trade agreements.

There are costs, benefits, and risks to both orientations. A free trade posture:

- Gives greater weight to economic efficiency, dynamism, and growth than to the job security of workers employed in import-competing industries;

- Facilitates U.S. diplomacy on other foreign policy issues;

- Requires significant amounts of political capital to implement; and

- Carries the danger of being viewed as uncaring toward Americans negatively affected by greater global competition.

Alternatively, a fair trade posture:

- Emphasizes economic security and the stability of import-competing sectors over economic efficiency, dynamism, and growth;

- Resonates strongly with the American public;

- Generates greater antagonism abroad toward U.S. foreign policy; and

- Carries the danger of mutating into blanket protectionism, severely weakening the global trading system and disrupting economic growth.

In a nutshell, the free trade orientation provides a more coherent set of economic policies, but carries a significant political risk. Adopting a free trade orientation will promote economic growth, keep a damper on inflation, and reaffirm U.S. economic leadership to the rest of the world. At the current moment, however, freer trade runs against the tide of public and congressional opinion; you risk the possibility of antagonizing the American public and being thwarted by congressional opposition. The fair trade orientation provides a more popular set of policies, but carries a significant policy risk. Adopting a tough position on slowing down imports while boosting exports will resonate strongly with many Americans. Because almost any trade barrier can be advocated on grounds of fairness to some group, however, special interests can easily hijack this policy orientation. Internationally, such a policy will be viewed as an abdication of U.S. economic leadership. Slowing down imports will encourage other countries to erect higher trade barriers against U.S. exports. Any kind of global trade war would severely damage the American economy—and American workers. In short, free trade is less difficult to negotiate but more difficult to sell at home, while fair trade is more difficult to negotiate but less difficult to sell at home.

Additional trade issues must also be addressed in the near term, such as regulatory coordination and the balancing of multiple tracks of trade diplomacy. These issues go beyond the free trade/fair trade dichotomy. There are multiple policy options to address these concerns; they are detailed in the white papers attached to this memo.

Why Trade Matters

Trade is vital to the U.S. economy for a number of reasons.

- In 1970, the sum of imports and exports was less than 12 percent of gross domestic product (GDP). By 2004, that figure had doubled to 24 percent.

- Approximately one out of every five factory jobs in the United States depends directly on trade, either by relying on export markets or by needing imported goods for final production.

- U.S. exports accounted for approximately 25 percent of economic growth during the 1990s, supporting an estimated 12 million jobs.

- U.S. farmers export one out of every three acres of their crops.

- In 2003, the United States exported $180 billion in high-tech goods and more than $280 billion in commercial services.

From agriculture to manufacturing to technology to services, the U.S. economy needs international trade to prosper. One recent analysis concludes that trade liberalization generates an additional $800 billion annually in national income for the United States; future trade expansion is estimated to benefit the U.S. economy by up to $1.3 trillion per year.

Trade is equally vital to American foreign policy.

- Trade will be essential to advancing the UN Millennium Development Goal of halving global poverty by 2015.

- The multilateral rules governing trade help spread the rule of law across the globe.

- Exposure to the global economy correlates strongly with the spread of democracy and the rule of law.

- Bilateral relations have improved with every country that has signed a free trade agreement with the United States.

The Current Trade Agenda
You have a full plate of trade issues for the next three years. At the top of the list is the suspended Doha round of WTO talks. We agreed at Doha, Qatar, in 2001 to work with the other 147 members of the WTO collectively to reduce trade barriers in order to promote economic development in poor countries. Disagreements between less-developed countries and the developed world threatened to derail the round at the WTO ministerial conference in Cancun in 2003. Our efforts reignited these talks in July 2004, and progress was made on a timetable for the elimination of agricultural export subsidies, flexibility on pharmaceutical patents, and the provision of development aid to encourage the least-developed countries to expand their trade.

Negotiations have stalled out, however, on the liberalization of trade in services, nonagricultural market access, and the reduction of internal price supports and market restrictions for agricultural producers. The original deadline for those negotiations was the Hong Kong ministerial conference in December 2005. That deadline came and went. Only marginal progress was achieved at the

Hong Kong ministerial conference or in follow-up negotiations in Geneva during the spring and summer of 2006. Negotiations were suspended in July 2006. There is a standoff between the EU, which does not want to reduce its internal agricultural supports any further, and the Group of Twenty advanced developing countries (G20), led by Brazil and India, which do not want to liberalize their industrial and service sectors. Both the EU and G20 have blamed the United States for the standoff, demanding that we lower our farm subsidies and agree to 100 percent market access for the least developed countries. As of this writing, the likelihood that the Doha round will be completed before the July 2007 expiration of the Trade Promotion Authority (TPA) that Congress granted to you is remote.

China presents the most vexing set of bilateral trade issues. As the February 2006 U.S. Trade Representative (USTR) review of the Sino-American trade relationship points out, there are disputes ranging from textile imports to corporate takeovers to the currency exchange rate. The end of the Multi-Fiber Agreement (which governed trade in textiles for more than three decades) on January 1, 2005, triggered a rush of textile and clothing imports from China—an increase of 29 percent in the first quarter of 2005. This surge of imports led to negotiations with Chinese authorities that placed temporary caps and tariffs on these goods. It also highlighted China's large bilateral trade surplus with the United States.

China has increasingly intervened in foreign exchange markets to maintain the dollar's value against the yuan, even though China's currency has recently risen in value compared to other major currencies. In July 2005, China's central bank announced a slight devaluation of the yuan against the dollar. Chinese officials also announced their intention to let the currency markets play a greater role in determining the exchange rate, within certain boundaries. All the available data, however, suggest that Beijing has continued to purchase large sums of dollars, ensuring that the yuan will not be appreciating any time soon. Beijing's interventions have exacerbated America's trade deficit with China, which in 2005 reached a record $201 billion.

These practices, combined with China's high growth rate, the media firestorm over offshore outsourcing, and the recent flurry of Chinese corporate takeover efforts directed at U.S. firms, have created intense domestic pressures for retaliation. In April 2005, a bill was introduced in the full Senate that threatened a 27.5 percent tariff on Chinese goods unless Beijing revalued its currency; as you know, the bill garnered a veto-proof majority. A different piece of legislation was proposed in the U.S. House of Representatives in May 2005 to widen the definition of exchange-rate manipulation to include China as an offender, which would trigger punitive trade sanctions. Many members of Congress reacted negatively to the proposed takeover of Unocal by the Chinese National Offshore Oil Corporation (CNOOC) in the summer of 2005. The House of Representatives passed a measure urging you to block the Unocal purchase on national security grounds. This congressional hostility helped to defeat CNOOC's takeover plans. Anxiety is nonetheless mounting about China's aggressive financing of and purchases of energy companies around the globe. Your decision on whether to adopt a free trade or a fair trade posture will dramatically affect how you cope with these domestic pressures.

At the regional level, we have most recently signed and implemented the Central American Free Trade Agreement (CAFTA) with six Central American countries. Both labor unions and environmental activists opposed CAFTA, arguing that the agreement lacks the regulatory safeguards present in other recent free trade agreements (FTAs), such as the Jordan Free Trade Agreement. As you know, CAFTA passed by only a two-vote margin in the House of Representatives. Efforts to advance the Free Trade Area of the Americas (FTAA) and the Middle Eastern Free Trade Area (MEFTA) initiatives are continuing, albeit at a much slower pace. At the bilateral level, we recently implemented FTAs with Australia and Morocco. We have ratified an FTA with

Bahrain, concluded FTAs with Oman and Peru, and negotiations with Panama, Colombia, Thailand, the United Arab Emirates, Malaysia, and South Korea are ongoing.

In the short term, your critical policy decision is to determine how much political capital to devote to the revival of the Doha round and to smoothing trade frictions with China. If you choose to adopt a free trade policy, your leadership will be required to complete the WTO negotiations in a timely fashion—and even then, it will not be easy to reconcile the positions of the various WTO constituencies and Congress. Similarly, it will require significant amounts of domestic political capital to prevent Congress and interest groups from forcing you to adopt a more hawkish U.S. foreign economic policy toward China. If you choose to adopt a fair trade policy, you will need to steer the negotiations toward a successful outcome while engaging in some tough bargaining with WTO partners. You will also need to find a way to exploit the domestic groundswell against China's foreign economic policy to extract trade concessions from that country—without going so far as to launch an all-out trade war that would harm the American economy. Your handling of these two issues will be the political signal that other world leaders and both houses of Congress will use to assess your intentions toward U.S. trade policy.

THE SHIFT IN DOMESTIC POLITICS

In the last five years, public support for free trade has plummeted at the same time that trade has become more salient to the American people. To some extent, the public has always been suspicious of free trade. For the past decade, more than 80 percent of Americans have consistently told the Chicago Council on Foreign Relations that protecting the jobs of American workers should be a top foreign policy priority. In recent years, however, the public has become even warier of trade expansion. The most dramatic shift in opinion came from Americans making more than $100,000 a year. According to the Program on International Policy Attitudes (PIPA), support in that income group for promoting trade dropped to 28 percent in 2004 from 57 percent in 1999. In July 2004, a German Marshall Fund of the United States (GMFUS) poll concluded that only 4 percent of Americans supported the North American Free Trade Agreement (NAFTA), which had been negotiated more than a decade earlier by the first Bush administration. Americans are also less enthusiastic about new international trade deals than are their European counterparts. A high proportion of Europeans—82 percent of the French and 83 percent of the British—want more international trade agreements, compared to just 54 percent of Americans.

Three political facts of life have caused many Americans to shift their support from free trade to fair trade. First, during tough economic times or times of economic uncertainty, public suspicion of free trade policies explodes into public hostility. Inevitably, foreign trade becomes the scapegoat for business-cycle fluctuations that have little to do with trade. When faced with a choice between economic theories and statistical data that show trade benefits the economy, and anecdotes of job losses due to import competition, Americans believe the anecdotes. There may be no correlation between trade and employment, but many Americans think that there is a relationship between the two—which means that there is a political relationship that policymakers ignore to their peril.

Second, it is particularly difficult to make the case for trade expansion during election years. Trade generates diffuse benefits but concentrated costs. Those who bear the costs are more likely to vote on the issue—and make campaign contributions based on the issue—than those who reap the benefits. In this situation, politicians will always be tempted to engage in protectionist rhetoric. The latest example of this came when concerns about offshore outsourcing sparked an outcry from many politicians on both sides of the aisle for government action to keep jobs in the United States. As members of Congress spend more and more time in campaign or fund-raising mode, this constraint will only get worse.

Third, both advocates and opponents simultaneously inflate the importance of trade while framing the issue as a zero-sum game. Trade is both blamed and praised for America's various economic strengths and ills, even though domestic factors—such as macroeconomic policy, the regulatory environment, and the pace of innovation—matter more for America's economic performance. Politicians routinely address trade issues by discussing how changes in policy will affect the trade deficit. The implicit assumption is that it is better to run a trade surplus, even though there is no correlation between the balance of trade and national income. Debates about trade inevitably revolve around the question of jobs—even though trade has a minimal effect on overall employment levels. Furthermore, this is hardly a recent phenomenon. A decade ago, the political debates over NAFTA were framed in terms of job creation and job destruction, despite the fact that every sober policy analysis concluded that NAFTA would not significantly alter the employment picture one way or the other. As a result, even politicians who advocate trade liberalization focus their rhetoric on increasing American exports while downplaying imports.

Public Opinion about Trade

Now that the economy has generated a net gain of nearly 2 million new jobs in the past year, the public should be more receptive to a discussion of free trade. Nevertheless, the fallout from the last economic downturn has dampened public enthusiasm toward freer trade. A September 2005 GMFUS survey revealed that 55 percent of polled Americans favor providing agricultural subsidies to large farms; 57 percent believe that freer trade destroys more American jobs than it creates; and 58 percent of Americans would favor raising tariffs for imported goods if it meant protecting jobs—a higher number than in Germany, France, or Great Britain. Healthy majorities believe that trade primarily benefits multinational corporations at the expense of small businesses.

Hostile attitudes toward trade liberalization are even more concentrated when the focus turns to newer forms of trade. In 2004 there was intense media focus on the practice of offshore outsourcing, which is when U.S. firms subcontract business services to overseas affiliates rather than having them done inside the United States. At least ten different surveys that year asked Americans how they felt about the growing number of jobs being outsourced overseas. The results were consistently and strongly negative. Depending on the poll, between 61 percent and 85 percent of respondents agreed with the statement that offshore outsourcing is bad for the American economy. Between 51 percent and 72 percent of Americans were in favor of the U.S. government penalizing American firms that engage in offshore outsourcing. In a Harris poll taken in May and June of 2004, 53 percent of Americans said American companies engaging in offshore outsourcing were "unpatriotic." A March 2006 Pew Research poll found 71 percent of Americans still believing that outsourcing was bad for the U.S. economy. This hostility remains consistent regardless of how the respondents are broken down: a *CFO Magazine* survey of chief financial officers revealed that 61 percent of them believed offshore outsourcing was bad for the economy; in an April 2004 Gallup poll, 66 percent of investors believed the practice was hurting the investment climate in the United States.

Even as the economy continues to add jobs, there are excellent reasons to believe that public antipathy toward trade liberalization will not abate; if anything, it will increase. While the public is perennially hostile to freer trade, until recently the issue was not important enough to mobilize political action. That could change over the next decade, as technological innovation will convert what were thought to be nontradable sectors into tradable ones. Trade will start to affect professions that have not changed their practices significantly for decades—such as accounting, medicine, education, and law. That will increase the number of Americans who perceive themselves to be vulnerable to international competition and economic insecurity.

Although these polls suggest a hostile political climate for trade expansion, this constraint may not be binding. To date, polling data, purchasing patterns, and experimental evidence all suggest that while American consumers talk like protectionists, they purchase goods like free traders. It is difficult to point to specific members of Congress who have lost their seats because they adopted an unpopular position on trade policy.

You have the ability, through both policy initiatives and the use of the bully pulpit, to change public attitudes. The primary impediment to boosting public support for trade liberalization is one not of economics but of psychology. People *feel* that their jobs and wages are threatened. Even if the probability of losing one's job from import competition or offshore outsourcing is small, the costs of losing one's job are great enough to provoke concern. Public-opinion polling strongly suggests that a healthy majority of Americans—including many skeptics of freer trade—support policies that pair liberalization with policies that help those hurt by trade. These policies can take the form of expanded benefits for displaced workers (such as wage insurance or health care portability), investment in public goods (such as basic scientific research and education), or retraining programs, among other possibilities. Nonetheless, some of the policy proposals discussed in this memorandum are likely to encounter stiffer resistance from the public than are others. Your involvement in shifting public attitudes will be needed to implement policies that run counter to opinion polling.

One of the reasons the United States was able to advance a trade liberalization agenda during the Cold War was the bipartisan consensus that a liberal trading system aided the cause of containment. Economic diplomacy served as America's first tool in the confrontation with communism. Likewise, trade expansion can and should be presented as a critical element of the long-term grand strategy of the United States to defeat terrorists and spread democracy. Security arguments resonate with a broad majority of the American public. As with the Cold War, a communications strategy that markets economic diplomacy as "America's first line of offense" would blunt the arguments of protectionists while promoting the virtues of trade liberalization.

Trade and Congress
The final restriction on advancing America's trade agenda comes from growing congressional constraints on the ability of the president to negotiate agreements with other countries. The U.S. Constitution gives Congress the power to set tariffs and trade policy. Since the Great Depression and the legacy of the 1930 Smoot-Hawley tariff, however, the legislative branch has recognized the need to bind its own hands in order to permit trade liberalization. That tariff was the most protectionist in history—in no small part because of logrolling among members of Congress to support raising individual tariffs on goods that affected their districts.

Since Smoot-Hawley, Congress has repeatedly granted the executive branch the authority to negotiate reductions in American trade barriers in return for reciprocal reductions by other countries. Starting in 1974, Congress granted the president "fast-track" authority for securing trade deals. This authority requires Congress to expedite consideration of trade deals submitted by the president under fast-track procedures, forbidding any amendments to the proposed trade agreements and requiring a straight "up-or-down" vote of approval in both houses of Congress.

The granting of fast-track authority, relabeled as TPA in 2002, enhances presidential credibility in multilateral trade negotiations. When foreign governments choose to enter into trade negotiations, or contemplate the extent to which they should open up their markets, they must evaluate the likelihood that the United States will honor its agreements. Without TPA, the likelihood that Congress will amend or revise a trade deal is high. TPA reassures other countries that the House and Senate will vote on the deal the White House actually negotiated, not the deal they wish it had negotiated.

As the post-NAFTA political climate for trade agreements has become more divisive, Congress has been increasingly reluctant to grant such authority to the president. From 1994 to 2002, Congress refused to pass TPA. As you may recall, that changed only because of the closest House vote in recent years—the December 2001 motion to grant you TPA, which passed by a single vote. In granting TPA in the Trade Act of 2002, Congress stipulated that U.S. trade negotiators participate in more detailed consultations with key congressional committees. It also placed more specific demands on trade negotiators in dealing with regulatory issues. Specifically, the 2002 act is the first legislation to require U.S. trade negotiators to give the same priority to the enforcement of environmental standards as they give to traditional negotiating aims. Anticorruption policies and unfair regulatory practices have also been added to the list of goals for trade negotiators to pursue. The act further mandates that the president consult Congress when negotiating trade deals that cover agriculture, fishing, and textiles.

Two arguments can be made in favor of increased congressional involvement in trade negotiations. First, the regulatory issues Congress incorporated into the trade agenda are not harmful to American interests in and of themselves; indeed, addressing many of these issues strongly resonates with the American public. Second, the changes to TPA enhance the transparency of the negotiating process. From a bargaining perspective, negotiators can exploit congressional pressure as a way of extracting concessions from other countries.

Yet there are two potential problems with the evolution of fast-track procedures. First, the principle behind TPA was to give presidents sufficient leeway to broker deals with other countries. As Congress adds additional negotiating mandates and inserts itself more vigorously into the negotiating process, America's trading partners may perceive its trade negotiators as inflexible. When the chairman of the House Ways and Means Committee gives a speech stating that the Doha round should be called off, it cannot make it easier to negotiate with our trading partners. Increased congressional influence on the negotiating process may make reciprocal reductions in trade barriers less likely in the short term, and over time this trend could sour other countries on negotiating with the United States in the first place. Even small states are reluctant to engage in (what are for them) costly and complex negotiations on sensitive trade issues without some assurance that American trade negotiators can honor the deals they make at the bargaining table.

Second, transparency is a double-edged sword. There is a trade-off between keeping Congress fully informed about and involved in the course of trade negotiations and the ability of negotiators to float trial balloons, propose cross-sectoral linkages, and engage in other bargaining strategies that facilitate agreements. Senators and representatives who oppose further trade liberalization will have an incentive to leak details of deals they dislike to labor unions, environmental groups, or other organizations in order to provoke political backlashes. The knowledge that draft texts and other bargaining-room details could become public puts an inevitable damper on the creativity that is often essential to achieving cooperative outcomes.

Even with TPA, the victory margins in congressional votes for FTAs have narrowed over the years, as Table 1 shows. The margins have been particularly thin with developing countries. CAFTA passed by only two votes in the House of Representatives, and that was after significant lobbying of wavering representatives by both you and congressional leaders. The smaller the margin of victory, the more leverage wavering representatives have to extract pork-barrel spending or trade-distorting measures that undercut the original purpose of the trade deal.

Table 1: Voting Results on Trade Bills Passed in the House of Representatives, 1993–2005

Year	Ref. no.	Title	Total Y	Total N	Democratic Y	Democratic N	Republican Y	Republican N
1993								
	HR 3450	NAFTA Implementation Act	234	200	102	156	132	43
1994								
	HR 5110	General Agreement on Tariffs and Trade	288	146	167	89	121	56
1997								
	HR 2644	U.S.-Caribbean Trade Partnership Act	182	234	46	150	136	83
1998								
	HR 2621	Reciprocal Trade Agreement Authorities Act	180	243	29	171	151	71
	HR 1432	African Growth and Opportunity Act	233	186	92	101	141	84
1999								
	HR 434	African Growth and Opportunity Act	234	163	98	99	136	63
2001								
	HR 3005	Bipartisan Trade Promotion Authority Act	215	214	21	189	194	23
2002								
	HR 3009	Andean Trade Preference Act	215	212	25	183	190	27
2003								
	HR 2738	United States–Chile Free Trade Agreement Implementation Act	270	156	75	128	195	27
	HR 2739	United States–Singapore Free Trade Agreement Implementation Act	272	155	75	127	197	27
2004								
	HR 4759	United States–Australia Free Trade Agreement Implementation Act	314	109	116	84	198	24
	HR 4842	United States–Morocco Free Trade Agreement Implementation Act	323	99	120	80	203	18
2005								
	H RES 57	Expressing the strong concern of the House of Representatives that the European Union may end its embargo against the People's Republic of China	411	3	190	2	220	1
	HR 3045	Dominican Republic–Central America–United States Free Trade Agreement Implementation Act	217	215	15	187	202	27

‡ Note: Discrepancies between "total," "Democratic," and "Republican" tallies reflect Independent voters.

A FREE TRADE APPROACH?

The free trade approach to trade policy assumes that the economic and political benefits reaped by the United States from multilateral trade expansion far outweigh the costs. The Institute for International Economics (IIE) recently attempted to measure the cumulative payoff from trade liberalization since the end of World War II. The IIE conservatively estimated that multilateral trade liberalization from 1945 to the present generates economic benefits ranging from $800 billion to $1.45 trillion dollars *per year* in added output. That translates into an added per capita benefit of between $2,800 and $5,000—an addition of somewhere between $7,100 and $12,900 per American household. The estimated gains from future trade expansion range between an additional $450 billion and $1.3 trillion per year in national income, which would increase per capita income between $1,500 and $2,000 on an annual basis. Few other options in the U.S. government's policy arsenal can yield rewards of this magnitude.

Adopting a free trade approach would mean the following:

- Reinvigorating American leadership in the Doha round of negotiations, by ensuring the involvement of you and your cabinet-level officers in bargaining with other countries;

- Demonstrating your willingness to make additional trade concessions (on lowering agricultural subsidies and allowing the temporary cross-border movement of foreign workers) within the context of the WTO talks to ensure a "deep Doha"—a round of negotiations that substantially liberalized trade in agriculture and services;

- Pursuing free trade agreements with major trading partners, such as India, South Korea, or Japan, if the Doha round fails to generate significant trade expansion;

- Pledging an all-out political push for the renewal of TPA in early 2007;

- Resisting congressional and interest-group pressure to punish China for the boom in Chinese textile imports;

- Resisting calls to block offshore outsourcing; and

- Convincing China to rethink its currency exchange-rate peg to the dollar without resorting to protectionist threats.

A Fair Trade Approach?

The fair trade approach to trade policy questions how ardently trade should be expanded. From a strictly economic perspective, it argues that conventional analyses underestimate the cost of job dislocation in an economy operating at less than full employment, and overestimate the benefits from trade liberalization. From a political perspective, it argues that trade policy needs to factor in values besides maximizing national income, such as community stability and income security. If trade expansion uproots community life or allows the importation of goods and services made in violation of American ethical norms, then these costs must be stacked against the undeniable economic benefits from trade. A fair trade approach argues that when social, moral, and political values are factored in, trade expansion benefits the United States only when such a policy is consistent with other American values. A fair trade doctrine further recommends using any and all safeguards, escape clauses, and other legal protections to limit job losses from import competition. At the same time, recognizing that export-related sectors yield higher-wage jobs, this doctrine advocates aggressively using all policy tools to expand export opportunities for U.S. firms and U.S. workers.

Adopting a fair trade approach would mean:

- Refusing to revive the Doha round of negotiations until developing countries and the European Union demonstrate a greater receptivity to American exports;

- Slowing down the number of bilateral free trade agreements signed with developing countries;

- Relying more on "managed trade" arrangements and unilateral trade sanctions to promote U.S. exports;

- Using escape clauses and safeguard mechanisms to slow the flood of Chinese textile imports into the United States;

- Implementing measures to retard the pace of offshore outsourcing; and

- Exploiting threats of protectionist action against China to force a substantial revaluation in the yuan.

THE CASE FOR A FREE TRADE APPROACH

The United States reaps significant economic and political advantages from expanding international trade opportunities. Adopting a free trade orientation toward China and the WTO would allow the United States to increase the size of these benefits.

The Economic Case for Freer Trade

Trade expansion produces four significant economic benefits for the United States. The principle of comparative advantage generates the most obvious benefit from trade—greater specialization. The idea behind comparative advantage is that even if one country is more productive at making every single good than another country, both economies would benefit from trade, because of improved division of labor. Trade allows the United States to specialize in making the goods in which it is the most productive, relative to other possible uses of resources. Economists from Adam Smith onward have pointed out that the bigger the market created from trade liberalization, the greater the benefits from specialization in areas of comparative advantage. Freer trade permits other countries to specialize as well. With freer trade, economies can increase economic output while holding inputs constant—in other words, trade creates a win-win arrangement for all participating economies.

The second benefit comes from increased competition within the same sector of production. Over the past several decades, economists have repeatedly shown that tradable economic sectors—i.e., those areas of the economy that produce goods or services that can be exchanged across borders—are more productive than sectors in which cross-border exchange is not possible. An open global economy dramatically expands market opportunities for both importers and exporters. With these opportunities comes greater competition, which forces firms to increase their efficiency. In an expanded market, individual firms—including multinational corporations—lack the market power to raise their prices above the market rate. Therefore, increased competition weakens the ability of companies to set prices. That translates into consumers paying lower prices while having more choice of goods.

The dynamic effect on economic growth is the third and perhaps most significant benefit from trade expansion. As available markets expand, the rate of return gained from technological and organizational innovations increases. Economists have long recognized that innovation is the single most important contributor to economic growth. With trade expansion, firms and entrepreneurs have a greater incentive to make risky investments in research and development (R&D). Trade expansion therefore significantly boosts economic growth. Furthermore, in some industries, such as the production of jumbo-sized commercial aircraft, a global market is necessary for a competitive market to exist.

The combined effect of these three benefits leads to the fourth benefit: the use of more expansionary monetary policies than would otherwise be possible (without triggering inflation). An open market is a significant reason why the United States has recently been able to sustain robust economic growth, dramatic increases in labor productivity, low rates of unemployment, modest rates of inflation, and historically low interest rates.

The Political Benefits of Freer Trade

The foreign policy benefits of an open trading system are significant. Trade expansion is vital to winning the global war on terrorism. Nine days after the September 11, 2001, terrorist attacks, your USTR argued,

> Economic strength—at home and abroad—is the foundation of America's hard and soft power. Earlier enemies learned that America is the arsenal of democracy; today's enemies will learn that America is the economic engine for freedom, opportunity, and development. To that end, U.S. leadership in promoting the international economic and trading system is vital. Trade is about more than economic efficiency. It promotes the values at the heart of this protracted struggle.

In April 2002, you made the following case in requesting TPA:

> Trade creates the habits of freedom. If you welcome trade into your country, it creates the notion of freedom. It gives people, consumers, the opportunity to demand product, which is part of a free society. It creates an entrepreneurial class, which is a part of a free society.
>
> And the habits of freedom begin to create the expectations of democracy and demands for better democratic institutions. Societies that open to commerce across their borders are more open to democracy within their borders. And for those of us who care about values and believe in values—not just American values, but universal values that promote human dignity—trade is a good way to do that.

Your September 2002 National Security Strategy (NSS) stated (and your March 2006 National Security Strategy reaffirmed),

> Poverty does not make poor people into terrorists and murderers. Yet poverty, weak institutions, and corruption can make weak states vulnerable to terrorist networks and drug cartels within their borders. The United States will stand beside any nation determined to build a better future by seeking the rewards of liberty for its people. Free trade and free markets have proven their ability to lift whole societies out of poverty—so the United States will work with individual nations, entire regions, and the entire global trading community to build a world that trades in freedom and therefore grows in prosperity.

A quick glance at the globe affirms these statements. The regions of the world that have embraced trade liberalization—North America, Europe, and East Asia—contain politically stable regimes and few incubators of terrorism. The regions of the world with the most tenuous connection to global markets—Africa and the Middle East—are plagued by unstable regimes and are hotbeds of terrorist activity.

Trade is not a silver bullet for U.S. foreign policy; many other factors affect the rise of terrorism and political instability. Nevertheless, trade is a handmaiden to hope and opportunity to individuals in poor countries, offering an improved quality of life for their children. Creating that kind of hope is a powerful weapon in the war against terrorism.

Beyond aiding the global war on terrorism, trade advances U.S. foreign policy interests in several ways. The most direct effect comes from poverty alleviation. Poverty, not trade, is the underlying cause of worker exploitation and environmental degradation in developing countries. These social ills are symptoms of a disease for which trade is the cure, not the cause. In the long run, the single best way to encourage developing countries to enforce workers' rights and protect the environment is to transform them into middle-income countries. Freer trade is an important mechanism through which the United States can assist in alleviating global poverty, because it provides an engine for economic growth in the developing world. Trade increases economic growth in developing countries; growth reduces poverty and its concomitant social ills.

Trade expansion directly and indirectly promotes democratic values by pushing countries toward policies that are compatible with democracy. For free trade to yield the greatest economic gain, governments must acquire a healthy respect for economic freedom, the rule of law, and well-defined property rights. These attributes are prerequisites of a functioning liberal democracy. Trade also contributes to greater income growth in poorer countries. By increasing economic growth, trade liberalization facilitates democratization, as wealthy countries are more likely to have stable democratic regimes. Among political scientists, it is a truism that freer trade, combined with international organizations and democratic institutions, reduces violent interstate conflict. Some studies go further, arguing that it is economic freedom itself that reduces the likelihood of war.

Trade expansion reduces domestic violence as well as interstate war. In the 1990s, the U.S. government–funded State Failure Task Force concluded that exposure to trade was one of three significant factors that helped to prevent the collapse of state authority. Evaluated according to accepted measures of economic and political freedoms, countries that are closed to trade are nine times more likely to suppress civil and political liberties. Statistical analysis reveals that countries agreeing to lower their trade barriers are more likely to respect human rights and labor rights within their borders.

For example, there is little doubt that the enactment of NAFTA locked Mexico onto a course of economic liberalization, but NAFTA also helped Mexico deepen its democratic institutions. The end of the grip of the Institutional Revolutionary Party (PRI) on the government occurred after NAFTA came into effect. The publisher of the newspaper *Reforma* observed after the fall of the PRI, "As the years have passed, with international mechanisms like NAFTA, the government doesn't control the newsprint, they don't have the monopoly on telecommunications, there's a consciousness among citizens that the president can't control everybody."

Even when the United States is not a direct participant in trade expansion, its foreign policy interests are served by the political reorientation and economic interdependence that trade can generate in other countries. The decision by western European governments to create the European Union has helped to preserve the peace on that continent after centuries of war and violence. Central and east European governments are less nationalist, more democratic, and more respectful of minority rights because they want to reap the economic benefits of EU membership. The Mercosur trade agreement helped cement democracy in the Southern Cone (Argentina, Brazil, Paraguay, and Uruguay); the agreement's provisions directly prevented a coup d'état in Paraguay in the late 1990s. The prospect of a South Asia Free Trade Area has caused both India and Pakistan to ratchet down their enduring geopolitical rivalry.

Trade can have a liberalizing effect even in countries that have yet to make the transition to democracy. China remains an authoritarian state ruled by a communist party, its government stands accused of multiple human rights abuses, and corruption is endemic. Nevertheless, China's accession to the WTO has helped to strengthen the rule of law in that country. China's economic openness has created a sizable, urbanized middle class. The Chinese Communist Party's Central Organization Department recently observed, "As the economic standing of the affluent stratum has increased, so too has its desire for greater political standing." This stratum is already lobbying for greater environmental protections—which in other ex-communist countries was a gateway to demanding greater political reforms. Trade has facilitated a Chinese society that is undeniably more open today than it was two decades ago.

Increasing America's trade with the rest of the world also generates useful tools of statecraft in the short and long runs. For the near future, freer trade combined with a growing American economy helps to foster export-led growth in other countries. Other countries rely on the U.S. market to sustain their own economic growth—creating opportunities for economic statecraft to advance our national interests. When used judiciously and diplomatically, the linkage between these economic relationships and American foreign policy preferences can help to nudge other governments toward policies that benefit the United States.

Over the long term, trade liberalization is a win-win proposition among countries and it therefore promotes American interests and values. Most of the time, trade acts as a foreign policy lubricant. If other countries perceive that the rules of the global economic game benefit all participants—and not merely the United States—these countries will be more favorably disposed toward the United States on other foreign policy dimensions. Over the very long term (i.e., the next several decades), U.S.-led trade expansion can cement favorable perceptions of the United States among rising great powers. Both the Central Intelligence Agency and private-sector analysts project that China and India will have larger economies than most members of the Group of Seven (G7), the world's leading industrialized nations, by 2030. Decades from now, it would serve American interests if these countries looked upon the United States as a country that aided rather than impeded their economic ascent. Trade liberalization with these countries now serves as a down payment for future good relations with rising great powers.

Again, it should be stressed that trade expansion is not a magic bullet that automatically leads to higher economic growth and greater political openness. Freer trade, economic growth, respect for human rights, democratic regimes, and a reduced likelihood of war all move in the same direction, and sometimes these other factors lead to freer trade rather than vice versa. Nevertheless, trade expansion is a useful policy tool.

THE CASE FOR A FAIR TRADE APPROACH

A fair trade approach argues that the benefits of free trade have been overstated, while its costs have been either understated or unobserved. A fair trade orientation intends to provide increased security for American workers while still looking for strategic openings for exports. The domestic political benefits of pursuing a fair trade doctrine must also be acknowledged.

This orientation should not be equated with simple protectionism. Fair traders recognize that trade expansion can yield positive results. They believe, however, that the conditions under which trade expansion benefits the American middle class are much narrower than free traders acknowledge.

The Hidden Costs of Trade Expansion

Freer trade is not costless. A vibrant, growing economy increases the churn of jobs: more jobs are created but more are destroyed as well. The logic of creative destruction implies some destruction in the national economy. Even free traders acknowledge this fact; according to an IIE estimate, the cost of trade expansion in terms of aggregate worker dislocation was estimated at $54 billion in 2003.

These costs may appear small when compared to the aggregate benefits reaped from trade, but they are quite large to the individuals who experience them.

Fair traders argue that international economists have consistently exaggerated the benefits and underestimated the costs that come with trade. Thirty years ago, economists estimated that the benefits of eliminating trade restrictions outweighed the costs of lost jobs by a factor of one hundred to one. However, a 2003 study concluded that economists have underestimated the loss resulting from job destruction—even when such losses are matched by job creation. Indeed, the benefit-cost ratio of trade expansion has been more like two to one.

Even that figure might overstate the benefits of trade expansion, though. The argument that trade does not lead to a net destruction of jobs is predicated on the assumption that the economy is always at full employment. The Economic Policy Institute estimates that, if this assumption is weakened, then trade with China alone has cost the United States more than 1.5 million jobs between 1989 and 2003. The Federal Reserve Bank of New York estimates that, in 2003, net imports embodied 2.6 million lost jobs. That number will only increase, given the growth in the trade deficit over the past few years and the projected growth of the deficit in the near future. A Carnegie Endowment for International Peace report argues that IIE and other free traders have overestimated the benefits that would come from a completion of the Doha round.

Just as significant as the stated economic costs are the psychological burdens that trade expansion can create. The psychological effects of losing a job cannot and should not be dismissed lightly. That is particularly true of trade-related job losses; once employment declines in import-competing sectors, it rarely bounces back. When import competition forces the shutdown of factories in rural areas, the costs of trade expansion affect communities across the board. The unusual nature of the current recovery—in which job creation has lagged significantly behind economic growth—has exacerbated the costs of these job losses.

Beyond job losses, another tangible cost of trade expansion is the effect trade can have on wages. Standard arguments in trade theory predict that, as the American economy opens up, workers in low-skilled jobs will suffer from wage suppression and greater income insecurity. This effect on wages increases as the number of tradable activities rises—that is, as more job seekers are competing against a global rather than a national supply of labor. All workers receive the benefit of lower consumer prices, but free trade clearly leaves some workers worse off in the short term. This concern about wages has been exacerbated in recent years. Despite the economic recovery that started in late 2001, for instance, a decreasing share of national income has gone to labor as opposed to capital, heightening class concerns that trade is increasing income inequality.

The United States could suffer economic losses from the opening of the global economy through the effects of worsening terms of trade. A country's terms of trade are estimated by how many exports are needed in order to purchase a given amount of imports. The greater the required amount of exports, the worse the terms of trade, which leads to lower real incomes. (By this logic, a depreciating currency, by worsening a country's terms of trade, depresses real incomes.) If a foreign country achieves technological progress in a U.S. export industry, it increases the supply and lowers the price of goods in that sector. Increased international competition in traditional export sectors deteriorates the terms of trade for the United States, rendering the U.S. economy worse off vis-à-vis the previous trade situation. Respected economists have recently voiced concern that developing countries such as China and India are moving up the productivity ladder and becoming increasingly competitive in high-value-added goods, forcing American exporters of such goods to lower their prices. If the United States loses its productive edge in these sectors, the effects on the U.S. terms of trade could reduce real incomes for all Americans. One rough estimate puts the loss of real income from this effect at 2 percent of GDP.

Another critique of free trade policies is that they have reduced U.S. bargaining leverage. At present, the U.S. economy is much more receptive to imports than are other economies. The average U.S. ad valorem tariff on manufactured imports is only 1.7 percent.[1] Seventy percent of manufactured imports enter the United States duty-free. In contrast, the National Association of Manufacturers (NAM) estimates that the average tariff imposed by a developing country on American goods exceeds 8 percent. Because developing countries receive "special and differential treatment" by the WTO, these countries have not had to open their markets as much to U.S. goods. However, the United States has opened up its market—with the WTO ensuring American compliance. WTO panels have never ruled in favor of the United States on cases involving the U.S. use of antidumping or escape-clause provisions.

Given the comparatively greater barriers to imports in other countries, the best course of action for the United States to maximize its benefits from trade is to push other countries—particularly those in the developing world—to reduce their explicit and implicit barriers to U.S. exports. While the best option in this regard would be to work within the WTO framework, no policy tool should be off the table. This approach would also provide substantial benefits to American workers; jobs in exporting plants pay wages up to 18 percent higher on average than jobs in nonexporting plants.

The International Political Costs of Trade Expansion
Free trade enthusiasts overlook three obvious foreign policy problems that come with trade expansion. The first comes from the antiglobalization movements. Since the December 1999 protests at the Seattle WTO ministerial meeting, protesters have targeted the WTO as the symbol of everything that is supposedly wrong with economic globalization. They have improved their coordination since Seattle, becoming the epitome of "smart mobs." A

---

[1]An ad valorem tariff on an imported good is a tariff determined in proportion to the value of the good.

well-organized antiglobalization movement generates two sets of costs for the United States. First, the protests themselves present logistical problems at important summit meetings, making it more difficult for the ministerial conferences to run smoothly. Second, the protesters have effectively spread their message that the WTO suffers from a "democracy deficit." According to this allegation, the WTO makes decisions of global import without any citizen input, making it a thoroughly undemocratic institution. If the Doha round ever comes to fruition, there will be considerable backlash from the antiglobalization movement.

A second and more serious foreign policy cost comes from the temporary social dislocations that trade expansion can generate in developing countries. Trade expansion contributes to a number of potentially disorientating trends in emerging markets. Export-led economic growth can increase income inequality, exacerbating pre-existing social tensions. Some scholars have argued that one trigger for ethnic violence in Southeast Asia in the 1990s was the expansion of trade, which increased inequality between "market-dominant minorities" and the majority of the population. The growth of export sectors in industrial areas also leads to mass migration from rural areas to urban shantytowns. Export growth can also lead more women to enter the formal employment sector. The economic empowerment of women, of course, is consistent with long-term U.S. interests and ideals. However, when this empowerment clashes with long-standing patriarchal structures in traditional societies, the political results can be dramatic. Globalization has facilitated the spread of communicable diseases such as severe acute respiratory syndrome (SARS) and avian flu, threatening to overwhelm the health care systems of poorer countries. In the developing world, government programs do not exist to cushion societies against these sorts of social shocks. Trade expansion by itself is unlikely to destabilize governments in developing countries, but combined with other factors, trade increases the fragility of these governments, creating foreign policy headaches for the United States.

The most problematic cost of a free trade policy is its effect on authoritarian regimes. Despite claims that trade is a lever that forces authoritarian countries to open up, fair trade advocates correctly point out that significant counterexamples exist. Singapore, for example, is a model of trade openness but remains a de facto one-party state.

The most prominent example of trade failing as a liberalizing force is China. There is little evidence that China's political culture has changed dramatically with increasing trade openness. By conventional measures of political freedom, such as the scale used by Freedom House, China has remained in the "not free" category for the past two decades despite significant economic opening. If anything, in recent years China's leadership has taken a harder line toward political dissent. For example, the communist government has been able to pressure Internet service providers and software manufacturers to censor or monitor subversive political content. Furthermore, China's growing economic size means that it can dictate terms to foreign companies eager to enter its vast market.

From a security perspective, China's economic growth and aggressive trade diplomacy pose significant challenges to the United States. In 2004, China accounted for 31 percent of global growth in the demand for oil. China's oil diplomacy has led to ambitious deals with Iran, Sudan, and Zimbabwe. Its growing inter-

Table 2: The Political Economy of Trade

	Domestic effects	**International effects**
Benefits from trade expansion	⬆ Greater economic growth Increased competition Greater consumer variety Flexible macroeconomic policy	⬆ Assists war on terrorism Promotes economic development Spreads democracy and the rule of law Improves bilateral relations
Costs from trade expansion	⬆ Greater economic insecurity Wage depression for low-skilled labor Worsening terms of trade	⬆ Exacerbates antiglobalization movement Fosters instability in developing countries Empowers authoritarian states

est in commercial relations with other Pacific Rim countries con-
trasts with U.S. regional policy, which prioritizes the global war
on terrorism. At a fundamental level, even if the United States benefits from the bilateral trading relationship, China appears to
benefit more—and that could clash with the stated NSS objec-
tive of "dissuad[ing] potential adversaries from pursuing a mili-
tary build-up in hopes of surpassing, or equaling, the power of the
United States."

The Benefits of a Fair Trade Approach
Beyond increasing economic security for workers in import-competing sectors, there is a final benefit that the fair trade orientation offers—it corresponds to the views of most Americans. As
previously observed, poll after poll suggests Americans want to see
the U.S. government place a higher priority on job protection. A
March 2006 poll sponsored by *Foreign Affairs* found a plurality
of Americans giving the government a failing grade for protecting their jobs from moving overseas. Pursuing a fair trade orientation would close the gap between what the public wants and what
the government actually does—it is, in other words, the more democratic policy choice.

THE DRAWBACKS OF THE FAIR TRADE ORIENTATION

The fair trade orientation amounts to a sustained critique of freer
trade. The problems with the fair trade orientation boil down to
two policy critiques: that it is impossible to draw a clear line
between fair trade and protectionism and that the international
response to the policies that fair traders favor would make it difficult if not impossible to negotiate a new global trade accord and
therefore jeopardize global economic growth and stability.

The fair trade orientation assumes that policymakers will be able
to discern when trade should be restricted because of concerns about
social dislocation and when it should not be restricted. In point

of fact, a fair trade orientation will encourage every special interest group to lobby harder for protecting its sector, using a fair trade argument to do so. It will become impossible to distinguish between groups that might need temporary protection and groups that are simply trying to prevent the market from working properly. Even if trade protection is applied in a judicious manner, once it is instituted it becomes politically next to impossible to remove. The first protections for the textile sector, instituted in the 1950s, were thought to be only temporary measures to ease the adjustment of workers into new sectors. A half-century later, the textile sector is still demanding and receiving "temporary" protections.

One way to appreciate the economic benefits of freer trade is to consider the converse: What is the outcome of greater protectionism? Fair traders argue that targeted protection preserves the jobs lost through import competition and offshore outsourcing. That statement is true, but it fails to consider the cost of this job preservation. The price for saving these jobs through trade barriers is that jobs are lost in sectors rendered less productive by higher input prices, higher consumer prices, lower rates of return for investors, and reduced incentives for innovation. Protectionist policies preserve jobs in less-competitive sectors of the economy and destroy current and future jobs in sectors that possess a comparative advantage. Trade protectionism amounts to an inefficient subsidy for uncompetitive sectors of the U.S. economy.

Two recent examples illustrate the costs of the fair trade approach. U.S. import quotas limit the amount of sugar the United States imports. As a result, U.S. sugar prices are 350 percent higher than world market prices. Although this policy has preserved a few thousand sugar-producing jobs, it has also cost an estimated 7,500 and 10,000 jobs, as candy makers relocated production to countries with lower sugar prices. Similarly, when the United States raised the tariffs on steel in 2002–2003, it raised the costs of production for steel-using sectors. Because steel users employ roughly forty times the manpower employed by steel producers, an estimated 45,000 to 75,000 jobs were lost.

There will also be a significant political cost to a fair trade orientation—the rest of the world will not see this orientation as particularly fair. Even though the leaders of India and Brazil are self-proclaimed socialists, they have rejected the idea that trade should be restricted in order to promote various forms of social and ethical regulation. These leaders have repeatedly stated that if altruistic motives are truly behind demands for tougher labor and environmental regulations, they would be pursued with tactics other than trade restrictions—such as strengthening the International Labor Organization (ILO).[2] Any move toward a fair trade orientation will give these countries carte blanche to erect their own protectionist barriers.

The instinct to block foreign trade and investment is present in countries beyond the United States. In the first half of 2006 alone, France and Luxembourg took steps to block Mittal Steel's takeover of the European conglomerate Arcelor. The French and Spanish governments took steps to prevent hostile takeovers of utilities from Italian and German firms, respectively. China's government has run into political roadblocks trying to pass a law reinforcing private property rights, with leftists accusing the government of excessive coziness toward foreign investors. In Latin America, socialist leader Evo Morales surged to victory in Bolivia's January 2006 presidential election after promising to renationalize the country's foreign-owned oil and gas concerns. In May 2006, he began implementing that policy, antagonizing Brazil and other countries in the process. In the same month, Ecuador followed suit, seizing Occidental Petroleum's oil and gas operations, leaving you no choice but to suspend FTA negotiations with that country. Argentinian president Nestor Kirchner, in response to rising domestic prices, instituted an export ban on beef—his county's main export—in March 2006.

A move toward protectionism by the United States carries the prospect of encouraging similar steps by other countries. A cas-

---

[2]See White Paper B for more on this topic.

cade of rising protectionism can lead to a drastic slump in international trade flows, increase financial instability, and depress the rate of global economic growth.

ADDITIONAL CHALLENGES TO THE TRADE AGENDA

In the current era of economic globalization, disentangling trade policy from other policy debates will become increasingly difficult. Numerous issues will pose obstacles to securing the benefits from international trade. These include—but are not limited to—the following:[3]

1. *Managing the trade deficit.* For the past several years, the United States has incurred a large trade deficit both in dollar terms and as a percentage of gross domestic product. Despite the growth of the deficit, and despite relatively low interest rates, the trade-weighted value of the dollar has not fallen by a large amount over the past few years. That combination has been possible because foreign central banks have been willing to purchase dollar-denominated assets in record amounts. These official purchases have been motivated by two concerns. First, Asian central banks have wanted to build up hard-currency reserves to ward off a repeat of the financial crises that swept the region in the late 1990s. Second, these countries have purchased U.S. assets to prevent their own currencies from appreciating. At this point, the first motivation has been satisfied. The second motivation, although still valid, cannot continue indefinitely, although how long it can be sustained is a source of debate among economists.

   When these official purchases taper off, the question is not whether the dollar will fall in value, but by how much and how fast. If the dollar were to decline dramatically, the effects on the U.S. economy—a combination of inflation and recession—could

---

[3]For more on these issues, see white papers A–D that follow this memorandum.

be severe. A drastic decline would also threaten the dollar's status as the global reserve currency—a status that confers significant benefits on the United States. It would also increase tensions with our major trading partners, since any dollar depreciation would act as a brake on their own economic growth. In a worst-case scenario, other governments will respond to rapid dollar depreciation by trying to devalue their own currencies—leading to the kind of beggar-thy-neighbor policies that were common during the Great Depression.

Ideally, market forces will lead to a slow and steady adjustment. However, you may need to consider active international policy coordination to hedge against a drastic decline in the dollar. That would include encouraging other countries to expand their economic growth as a way of boosting U.S. exports, while simultaneously reducing the budget deficit as a way of reducing the inflow of imports.

2. *Trade and regulation.* Because of the WTO's relative success in reducing tariffs and quotas, your trade negotiators are focusing more on domestic regulation as a residual barrier to trade expansion. At the same time, technology has expanded the range of tradable sectors. These newly tradable activities are subject to extensive domestic rules and regulations in most jurisdictions. These two facts are forcing trade policy to intersect with a range of other issue areas, the most obvious of which include labor standards, environmental protection, consumer health and safety, antitrust, intellectual property rights (IPR), and immigration controls.

Given the intersection of trade and regulatory concerns, both the European Union and nongovernmental organizations (NGOs) want the WTO adjudicating bodies to incorporate new, nontraditional issues into their decision-making. Yet, creating ambitious "social clauses" within the WTO structure will be difficult because less-developed countries view regulatory concerns as a guise for first-world protectionism.

Most regulatory policies were originally devised as domestic policies, so they are more politically difficult to change than tariffs or quotas. The more that trade policy intersects with these new issues, the harder it will become to implement effective trade policies. It will also become difficult to resist the linkages entirely.

3. *Distributing the benefits from trade.* Economists agree that trade creates individual winners and losers, and that the net benefits are great enough for the winners to compensate the losers and still be better off than before. Most policy analysts would agree that the compensation mechanisms in the United States do not meet that standard. For example, the best-known mechanism for offsetting the harmful effects of trade liberalization in the United States is the Trade Adjustment Assistance (TAA) program. Yet despite reforms in 2002, service-sector workers face near-insuperable hurdles in applying for TAA, even though trade in services has boomed in the past decade. Implementation of TAA programs has been uneven across different U.S. government agencies.

There are possibilities for augmenting TAA, such as expanding wage-insurance programs that allow displaced workers to seek new jobs or receive portable health benefits. However, there is a trade-off with expanding other elements of TAA. They reduce the incentive of the affected individuals to reenter the workforce. Furthermore, an expansion of benefits would raise questions about why compensation for job losses via trade should receive more resources than job losses via other market forces. Reforms in this area must convince Americans that trade expansion does not harm the majority of workers, without removing the incentives for displaced workers to look for new employment.

4. *Balancing the parallel tracks of trade diplomacy.* Over the past two decades, trade liberalization has advanced on three fronts— the multilateral process of General Agreement on Tariffs and Trade (GATT) and now WTO rounds, regional and bilater-

al FTAs that go beyond the WTO process, and unilateral measures designed to pressure foreign markets to widen their access to U.S. exports. The unilateral, bilateral, and regional options have often been used to spur movement on the multilateral track. For example, the simultaneous diplomacy of negotiating NAFTA and aggressively threatening to use unilateral trade sanctions demonstrated that the United States had a fallback option in case the Uruguay round of GATT talks did not go as planned. In that way, these strategies can be complementary.

Yet it is debatable whether the current mix of these negotiating strategies remains complementary. Beyond the FTAA (on which negotiations came to a standstill after the November 2005 Summit of the Americas in Mar del Plata, Argentina), none of the FTAs currently being negotiated provide the same negotiating leverage vis-à-vis the WTO (though the proposed FTA with South Korea is an exception). That is not to say that these FTAs are purposeless. Many of them serve useful foreign policy goals, such as buttressing the Greater Middle Eastern Peace Initiative. Other FTAs serve to advance U.S. concerns about labor rights or anticorruption policies.

The importance of the Doha round—and of the WTO more generally—to U.S. trade policy raises a question about how you wish to allocate U.S. efforts among the unilateral, bilateral, regional, and multilateral negotiation tracks. You could choose to prioritize political and foreign policy concerns first and focus on extending preferential trade access to vital allies in the war on terrorism. A second possibility is for you to impose an unofficial moratorium on future FTAs until the substantive negotiations on the Doha round have been completed. A final possibility is for your administration to concentrate on FTAs with significant trading partners—such as South Korea, Japan, or the European Union—as a way of jumpstarting the stalled Doha round negotiations.

RECOMMENDATION

Trade can be a means to several ends—raising incomes, expanding consumer choice, helping poor countries develop, promoting the rule of law, and advancing American foreign policy. The expansion of international trade offers several benefits but also comes with economic and political costs: economic insecurity, slower wage growth, widening inequality, and instability in the developing world. The big questions facing your administration in the near term are the extent to which you are prepared to bring the now-moribund Doha round to a successful conclusion, and how you want to address the bilateral trading relationship with China. Your trade agenda will face additional challenges over the next two years, such as the enmeshing of trade and regulatory concerns, the ballooning trade deficit, the trade-offs between different negotiation tracks, and the distribution of benefits from trade expansion. Trade policy can no longer be forged without taking into account these other policy concerns.

We urge you to pursue a course of trade expansion consistent with either the free trade or the fair trade orientation outlined in this memo. We recommend that you convene a meeting of your principal economic and foreign policy advisers, using this memo and the background white papers that accompany it as guidance for discussions. After soliciting feedback on the options developed here, you should arrive at a single orientation to shape your trade agenda for the next two years.

Table 3: The Policy Matrix	
Policy problem	**Menu of policy options**
Trade deficit	⬆ Bring Article XXIV cases to WTO to prevent trade diversion Initiate forceful exchange-rate diplomacy via the IMF Encourage growth-promoting policies in export markets Encourage efforts to reduce energy dependence Implement contractionary fiscal policies Encourage carrot-and-stick diplomacy on exchange rates, with a particular emphasis on China Restrain growth in government spending Rely on market forces to adjust exchange rates
Trade and regulation	⬆ Attempt to expand use of regulatory exceptions in GATT articles; as fallback, expand use of Generalized System of Preferences leverage to extract progress on labor, environmental issues Demand service liberalization in countries that are large beneficiaries of offshore outsourcing Expand funding and mandate of the Standards and Trade Development Facility and the Integrated Framework for Trade-Related Technical Assistance Focus on bilateral and regional agreements as a way to widen U.S. "regulatory bloc" Resist adding these issues to WTO bailiwick Rely on market forces, bolster non-WTO bodies to alleviate regulatory concerns Launch Regulatory Impediments Initiative with the EU
Distribution of benefits	⬆ Enforce antidumping, countervailing duty measures more aggressively Require firms to increase advance warning of job displacements Expand Trade Adjustment Assistance benefits to cover service-sector workers Equalize bureaucratic efforts and public outreach to service Trade Adjustment Assistance recipients Expand tax incentives to promote private wage insurance schemes Expand buyout programs for agricultural landowners Expand public investments in education and basic research
Balancing the negotiation tracks	⬆ First option: enforce multilateral rules; fallback option: encourage unilateral trade diplomacy First option: expand the WTO's purview to address regulatory concerns; fallback option: expand the number of regional and bilateral free trade agreements First option: focus on trade liberalization through the WTO; fallback option: initiate free trade agreements with major trading partners—i.e., South Korea, Japan, EU

WHITE PAPER A: THE SUSTAINABILITY OF THE TRADE DEFICIT

THE STATE OF THE TRADE DEFICIT

The United States is running a massive trade deficit. The United States ran an $804.9 billion current account deficit in 2005—a 20 percent increase over the 2004 number, which was in turn a 20 percent increase over the 2003 figure. In absolute dollar terms, these are the largest trade deficits in world economic history.

Trade deficits are not necessarily bad for the American economy. Robust economic growth leads to greater consumer demand. Even if the lion's share of this increased consumption goes into domestically produced goods and services, a fraction of it will inevitably take the form of increased imports. Since American economic growth has little short-term effect on the purchasing power of other countries, the natural outcome is a larger trade deficit. Not surprisingly, since 1998 the growth in the U.S. trade deficit has been accompanied by strong GDP growth and excellent productivity gains. That suggests, at first glance, that a large trade deficit could be a natural equilibrium for a robust economy.

A large and persistent deficit in traded goods and services, however, cannot be sustained indefinitely, because it requires foreign investors—public or private—to purchase an ever-increasing amount of dollar-denominated assets. The question, therefore, is not whether the trade deficit will start to shrink, but how and when. One possibility is that market forces will lead to a gradual adjustment even without any policy intervention by the U.S. government. Yet the likelihood of severe economic dislocations cannot be dismissed. There are policy options available to reduce the probability that the trade deficit will trigger inflation, recession, or a run on the dollar.

DEFINING THE TRADE DEFICIT

The balance of trade is equal to the value of the goods and services the United States imports minus those goods and services the United States exports. The United States currently has a trade deficit because the value of goods and services imported exceeds the value of the goods and services exported.

In everyday terminology, the trade balance is commonly equated with the current account balance, but that is not completely accurate. The current account balance is equal to the trade balance plus the net transfer of interest payments, labor remittances, and aid transfers. Even countries with positive trade balances can run large current account deficits for an extended period of time if they have significant amounts of inward portfolio and direct foreign investment—i.e., foreigners investing in the stock market or setting up physical plants in the United States. However, if the cause of a large current account deficit is a large trade deficit, then the current account deficit would inevitably start to balloon in size. Trade deficits are financed by the purchase of American assets by foreigners. Over time, trade deficits of the magnitude we are currently experiencing require massive foreign purchases of interest-bearing assets in the United States. These purchases finance the trade deficit in the short run but could accelerate the growth of the current account deficit in the long run by increasing interest payments to foreign asset holders.

The data in Figure 1 demonstrate the extent to which the current account deficit is unprecedented by historical standards—both in terms of absolute size and as a percentage of GDP. Ironically, one initial cause of the growth in the trade deficit was a dramatic increase in the capital account surplus. In the late 1990s, private foreign capital rushed into the United States, because American capital markets served as a safe haven from the Asian financial crisis, and U.S. capital markets were exhibiting above-average rates of return. That led to a strong appreciation of the dollar, which caused the trade deficit to widen.

WHY HAS THE TRADE DEFICIT PERSISTED?

In theory, when a country runs a large trade deficit with a floating exchange rate, one of two mechanisms should reduce the deficit. The first option is tightening fiscal policy, either through reduced government spending or increased tax rates. This contracts the economy, boosts national savings, and reduces the demand for imports. The other option is to let market forces work through the exchange rate. When the United States runs a large trade deficit, it means that Americans are demanding foreign currencies more than foreigners are demanding the dollar. The market response is for the dollar to fall in value relative to other currencies. A depre-

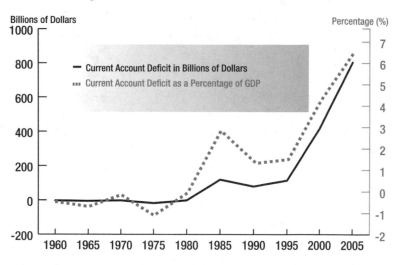

Figure 1. Growth of the Current Account Deficit

Source: U.S. Department of Commerce: Bureau of Economic Analysis; see http://www.bea.gov/bea/di/home/bop.htm for balance of payments and http://www.bea.gov/bea/dn/nipaweb/TableView.asp#Mid for gross domestic product.

ciating dollar renders imports more expensive and exports cheaper. That leads to an improved balance of trade, ostensibly fixing the problem.

The anomaly of the past five years is that neither of these equilibrating mechanisms has really taken hold. Government spending has increased and tax rates have declined; during these same years, the U.S. trade deficit nearly doubled in size. Until recently, interest rates in the United States were at a historic low. In 2004 alone, outward private foreign investment exceeded inward private investment by $500 billion. The dollar remains strong compared to the euro, the Japanese yen, the Chinese yuan, and other major currencies. Indeed, when compared against a weighted index of other currencies, the dollar's value was higher at the end of 2004 than it was in 1997.

There are several possible explanations for the dollar's anomalous behavior. One is official interventions by central banks, particularly by Pacific Rim and oil-exporting countries. Starting in 2000, private capital inflows to the United States slowed down. The central banks of Japan, China, and other East Asian economies began to purchase enormous amounts of dollars. From 2000 to 2003,

Figure 2. Change in Exchange Rate of U.S. Dollar, 1999–2006

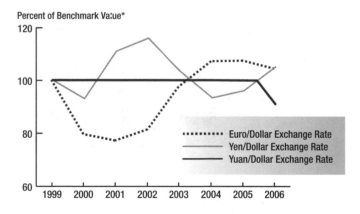

*The "benchmark value" is the value of one U.S. dollar in each currency in January 1999, the first month after the changeover to the euro.
Source: Federal Reserve Bank of St. Louis; see http://research.stlouisfed.org/fred2/categories/95.

the official share of foreign investment flows into the United States increased from 4 percent to 30 percent. As oil prices increased, countries such as Russia and Saudi Arabia recycled their petrodollars by purchasing U.S. assets.

One initial explanation for these purchases was that the East Asian countries wanted to build up their hard currency reserves, which had been badly depleted during the financial crises of the late 1990s. Countries harmed by the crisis—such as South Korea— have been intent on ensuring that they have built up sufficient funds to prevent a return visit to the International Monetary Fund (IMF). In recent years, however, the underlying cause of these dollar purchases has been to keep these countries' currencies under- valued relative to the dollar.

That tactic has led to a massive accumulation of foreign exchange reserves by central banks in China, Japan, India, Korea, and other Asian countries, as Table 4 demonstrates. IMF data states

Figure 3. Foreign Purchases of Dollar Reserve Assets

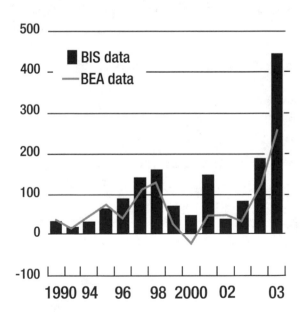

Source: Bank for International Settlements; Bureau of Economic Analysis.
Reproduced from *Financial Times,* February 23, 2005.

that the hard currency reserves of central banks have doubled in the past four years and now stand at a combined total of over $4 trillion. In that time, the Central Bank of Japan increased its reserves by over 200 percent and China's reserves increased by almost 400 percent. The stock of official Chinese reserves at the end of 2005 has been estimated at approximately $822 billion, equal to almost 40 percent of China's GDP at market exchange rates. In total, foreign official holdings account for 16 percent of all foreign-held assets in the United States; this includes more than $1 trillion in U.S. Treasury securities. These purchases allow those countries' currencies to remain undervalued vis-à-vis the dollar.

A less pernicious explanation for the dollar's refusal to fall is that a global savings glut is channeling significant investment into the United States. According to this line of reasoning, some countries have renewed incentives to save a high fraction of their income. Countries such as Japan and Germany are saving because of the increase in pensioners, while countries such as China and Korea are saving in response to the crisis-ridden 1990s, and countries such as Saudi Arabia and Russia are saving because of profits from high energy prices and a need to recycle their petrodollars. The lack of desirable domestic investment opportunities has funneled this money into safe investments in the United States—including government debt and housing stock, which has fueled U.S. consumer spending. According to this line of reasoning, foreign investors are pushing Americans into greater consumption, and not vice versa.

Table 4: Foreign Exchange Reserves		
Country	Foreign exchange reserves (in billions)	
	December 1998	December 2005
Japan	$215	$834
China	$149	$822
Korea	$52	$210
Russia	$8	$176
India	$27	$132
TOTAL	**$451**	**$2,174**

SCENARIOS FOR THE FUTURE

Although the dollar appreciated by 10 percent in 2005, economists agree that inevitably the dollar will fall in value, leading to an improvement in the balance of trade. What economists cannot predict is the speed and extent of this market correction. One possibility is a soft landing, in which the United States does not shoulder a great deal of the burden. As the dollar falls relative to the euro, America's trade position should slowly improve. To protect their dollar holdings, East Asian central banks would taper off their purchases of dollar assets slowly rather than suddenly. Over time, the trade deficit would fall without any excessive volatility for the American economy (indeed, under this scenario, the eurozone would suffer the greatest economic costs).

The other scenario is an abrupt end to official dollar purchases by foreigners. The dollar's fall in value relative to the other principal reserve currency—the euro—will be costly for the central banks holding large amounts of dollar-denominated assets. In purchasing so many dollars, these banks have a powerful incentive to ensure that their investment retains its value—but they have an equally powerful incentive to sell off their reserves if it appears that the dollar will rapidly depreciate. The Federal Reserve Bank of New York recently calculated that Singapore would suffer capital losses equivalent to one-tenth of its GDP if its currency rose by 10 percent against the dollar. For China and Korea, the cost of such an appreciation would be 3 percent of their GDP. In a late 2004 survey, 70 percent of central bank reserve managers said they had increased their exposure to the euro over the past year—and a plurality indicated that they intended to slow down their accumulation of official reserves (that said, the persistence of official purchases in the past calendar year does call into question those survey responses).

The potential cost of a sliding dollar creates a dilemma for these central banks. Collectively, these central banks have an incentive to hold and purchase more dollars, so as to maintain the dollar's value on world currency markets. Individually, each central bank has an incentive to sell dollars and diversify its holdings into other hard currencies because of the expectation that the dollar will fall in value in the future. Small countries—such as the United Arab Emirates—have already diversified their reserves away from dollars. The resulting fear of defection leads to a classic prisoner's dilemma—and the risk that these central banks will simultaneously try to diversify their currency portfolios poses the greatest threat of a run on the dollar. Like a run on a bank, a run on the dollar would take place if foreign actors holding significant amounts of dollars simultaneously tried to sell them. At present, currency markets are primed for this possibility. For example, in February 2005, an official Bank of Korea report hinted at the possibility of diversification of its official currency reserves. That vague statement helped trigger a massive sell-off of dollars, causing the dollar to fall 1.4 percent against both the yen and the euro in a single day. Only after the Koreans issued a clarifying statement did dollar demand recover.

Any decision by the major central banks to sell off dollars would make it impossible to finance the current account deficit at current price levels and interest rates. Under this worst-case scenario, a run on the dollar could commence. A drastic fall in the dollar's value would fuel inflation at home as the prices of imports shot up. The Federal Reserve Board would in all likelihood ratchet up the short-term federal funds rate in order to stanch outward capital flows. The result would be severe stagflation—higher prices combined with decreased output. At a minimum, such a move would trigger a severe economic slowdown.

A run on the dollar could also cause a shift in the allocation of central bank reserves and global accounting, with the dollar losing its status as the world's reserve currency. That would cost the United States the benefits that come with seigniorage—the profit that the government derives from the sale of American currency—which are currently estimated to range between $25 billion and $50 billion per year. At present, the dollar functions as the reserve currency in the global marketplace, so both private and public financial institutions in other countries are obliged to hold some of their assets in the form of dollars. Because these dollars are never intended to be put into circulation, the U.S. government earns a profit from their use—in the form of foreign exchange reserves. If the dollar were to lose its status as the reserve currency, the demand for dollar reserves among foreign financial institutions would dry up, drastically reducing seigniorage profits.

HOW TO SHRINK THE TRADE DEFICIT

The trade-off between maintaining economic growth and reducing the risk of a run on the dollar is unavoidable. If the paramount concern is lowering the probability of worst-case scenarios for the dollar, then the United States needs to pursue policies that allow market forces to work without increasing uncertainty or volatility. The most salient policy option is to persuade Japan, China, and other Pacific Rim countries to let their currencies slowly appreciate against the dollar. The regional trade imbalance between the United States and the Pacific Rim is so great that a change in the exchange rate between the dollar and these currencies would have the most direct effect on the U.S. trade deficit.

Of course, these countries will resist such a proposal. They oppose any revaluation of their currencies, in part because it would reduce the value of their foreign exchange portfolio. More important, their dollar purchases function as a subsidy to their exporters and help to sustain these countries' economic growth. One way to ease the pain is to encourage these countries to substitute domestic consumption for export subsidies as a mechanism for growth. However, the last time that the Pacific Rim countries encouraged domestic consumption and investment was the period leading up to the Asian financial crisis—making them wary of that approach.

The only way this strategy will yield results is if the United States is able to convince China and Japan to agree to revaluation of their currencies. These countries are the largest economies in the region and also the largest holders of dollar reserves. The question is, What incentives can the U.S. government offer to ensure cooperation on this front?

Gaining an agreement on revaluation will be particularly difficult with regard to China. Although the Chinese Central Bank announced steps in July 2005 to move toward a managed float of the yuan, actual currency movements suggest that the government is continuing to intervene on a massive scale to prop up the dollar's value. At present, China's financial sector is too fragile to let the yuan truly float. Indeed, if the yuan were allowed to float freely, it could *fall* against the dollar as private Chinese investors tried to move their assets into the United States in order to preserve their property rights. China is also benefiting from an influx of foreign investment in anticipation of an inevitable appreciation of the yuan.

THE POLICY OPTIONS

Your policy options on this issue depend on the emphasis you place on government intervention to correct the current macroeconomic imbalance. An interventionist platform would advocate a mix of internal and external policies to reduce the most glaring bilateral trade deficits—specifically, those with the countries of the Pacific Rim and the members of the Organization of Petroleum Exporting Countries (OPEC).

With regard to East Asia, the first interventionist policy recommendation would be for you to press the IMF to actively enforce its own rules. East Asian central banks are intervening in currency markets to keep their currencies at fixed exchange rates that are no longer in alignment with real exchange rates. The persistent and one-sided nature of these interventions renders this activity distinct from the standard currency-market interventions that are associated with a fixed-exchange-rate regime. The IMF's Articles of Agreement (Article IV, section 1, paragraph iii) specifically warn member countries against "manipulating exchange rates or the international monetary system in order to prevent effective balance of payments adjustment or to gain an unfair competitive advantage over other members." One could argue that Japan and China have violated both the letter and the spirit of that agreement by preventing market forces from readjusting the dollar's trade-weighted value. The IMF managing director should call for ad hoc consultations with both countries on this issue. Such a maneuver is extremely rare but not unprecedented, and it would send a powerful signal to these countries about the seriousness of their infraction.

A related proposal would be to urge other countries to pursue more expansionary macroeconomic policies at home. Although that has been the persistent U.S. position at meetings of the G7, the message should also go to the emerging market economies that form the Group of Twenty. Part of the reason the United States is running a large deficit is that consumption in other countries has been growing at a sluggish pace. In contrast, U.S. consumption has recently been so strong that 2004 produced the highest rate of global growth in a decade. It is an unbalanced recipe for sustained global growth. If the U.S. economy slows down, other countries will need to pick up the slack to prevent a global recession. In the process, the U.S. trade deficit will be reduced, as faster growth in other countries would translate into more U.S. exports.

You took the necessary first steps in the policy process at the Spring 2006 IMF/World Bank meetings in Washington. At those meetings, the G7 and other major economies agreed to have the IMF take the lead in consulting on correcting global economic imbalances. The communiqué stated that, "action for orderly medium-term resolution of global imbalances is a shared responsibility.... The agreed policy strategy to address imbalances remains valid. Key elements include raising national saving in the United States—with measures to reduce the budget deficit and spur private saving; implementing structural reforms to sustain growth potential and boost domestic demand in the euro area and several other countries; further structural reforms, including fiscal consolidation, in Japan; allowing greater exchange rate flexibility in a number of surplus countries in emerging Asia; and promoting efficient absorption of higher oil revenues in oil-exporting countries with strong macroeconomic policies." Achieving successful policy coordination on this scale is an ambitious undertaking. However, at least the major economic powers agree that the source of the problem is not limited to the United States.

Another way to improve U.S. exports would be to halt the trade diversion created by the European Union's preferential trade agreements with most of the rest of the world. These preferential arrangements often divert existing trade flows rather than create any trade expansion, making them economically inefficient and contradictory to the spirit of the WTO. Consistent with the doctrine of ensuring that multilateral institutions enforce their own rules, your administration could file complaints at the WTO that many of these preferential trade agreements violate Article XXIV of GATT, which states "the purpose of such agreements should be to facilitate trade between the constituent territories *and not to raise barriers to the trade of other members* [emphasis added]." Ideally, such a tactic would force the European Union and other jurisdictions to lower their barriers to American-made goods.

Another long-run option to manage the trade deficit that many outside policy analysts have embraced is to reduce America's appetite for imported oil. In 2005, oil and petroleum products were responsible for one-third of America's trade deficit. Oil prices have increased to near-record levels, and the U.S. reliance on foreign imports has also increased. The Department of Energy (DOE) estimates that imports account for 59 percent of total U.S. oil consumption at present. It does not expect that figure to be any lower by 2025. In the wake of a devastating 2005 hurricane season, your administration urged Americans to conserve energy. Historically, however, such moral exhortations have had little practical effect on consumer behavior.

Expanding domestic sources of energy through exploration in the Arctic National Wildlife Refuge (ANWR), increased incentives for alternative energy sources, and reduced regulatory burdens for extraction and refining activities is one option. Another would be to encourage conservation through a variety of incentives or regulations, such as enhancing fuel-efficiency standards for automobiles and sport-utility vehicles, increased funding for fuel-cell technologies, eliminating barriers to ethanol imports, and offering deeper tax incentives for the purchase of hybrid cars. It would take several years for ANWR to generate any appreciable amount of oil, or for alternative energy sources to come online, but instituting these policies now would help ensure a level playing field in the future. Some of these proposals are contained in your Advanced Energy Initiative.

If you prefer government action but are reluctant to adopt some of the higher-risk options discussed above, you still have other available strategies. One option is to rhetorically stress the interdependent nature of the U.S. trade deficit. Although America's demand for imports has fueled part of the trade deficit, the sluggish growth in domestic consumption in the rest of the world is another significant factor. This lack of growth has led countries in the Pacific Rim to depend excessively on U.S. aggregate demand to sustain their economies. If the United States should pursue a contractionary macroeconomic policy to reduce the demand for imports, the effect will reverberate around the world. More specifically, U.S. negotiators can plausibly argue that a yuan-dollar revaluation would help China in several ways. Having China revalue the yuan would ease protectionist pressures in the United States. Such a move would also be an effective way to slow down Chinese economic growth, lowering worries in that country about inflation, environmental devastation, and the rush of inward investment designed to capitalize on the anticipated revaluation of the yuan.

That leads to the second strategy: linking U.S. macroeconomic policy to China's and Japan's willingness to revalue their currencies. The less these countries accommodate the United States by making exchange-rate adjustments, the more the Federal Reserve Board will be forced to raise interest rates, and the more

U.S. government spending will have to be curtailed. Both revaluation and contractionary macroeconomic policies will slow East Asian growth. However, the advantage of a coordinated revaluation is that it provides more certainty and control for all the affected governments.

The United States could offer China the carrot of greater consultation with the G7 finance ministers and central bank chairs. This process started in the fall of 2004, when China's finance minister and central bank governor were invited to an informal meeting with the parallel officers from the G7 members. Permitting greater Chinese participation in some aspects of the G7 process would serve the interests of the United States in facilitating coordinated exchange-rate adjustments when necessary. Such a move would also be viewed positively by China as a signal of its emerging status both as a great power and as a locomotive for the global economy. Giving China a greater sense of "ownership" of the G7 process would also nudge that country toward a more cooperative attitude.

A final gambit would be to link China's status as a "nonmarket economy" in U.S. antidumping laws to greater flexibility on exchange rates. From 2001 to 2004, China was the target of thirty-two antidumping investigations by the Commerce Department's Import Administration—nearly three times as many as the next most targeted country. Under Article VI of GATT, nonmarket countries can be treated differently to determine whether firms from those countries are selling goods to the United States at below-market value. As a result, Chinese sectors found to be dumping have faced an average tariff increase of 112.85 percent—three and a half times the average penalty for producers in market economies. A partial switch in China's situation—market economy status for appropriate sectors—could be proffered in exchange for a revaluation.

You and your advisers can also decide that the current balance-of-payments situation does not justify added diplomacy. Although the official financing of the trade deficit cannot continue indefinitely, it may continue for a longer period of time than many economists believe. It is possible, for example, that existing trade figures are not capturing all U.S. exports. Despite the fact that foreigners own an increasing amount of U.S. assets, the flows of interest on investment income continue to favor the United States. For example, foreigners currently have a net claim on $2.5 trillion in U.S. assets, but the United States earned $36 billion more on their foreign investments than foreigners earned in the United States in 2005. That is partially due to foreigners investing in lower-risk assets—but it is also because U.S. foreign direct investment abroad earns a much higher rate of return than foreigners' foreign direct investment in the United States. This difference in profit rates has persisted for decades. Some economists believe that these numbers reveal a hidden U.S. export—American managerial expertise and knowledge. Other economists go further, characterizing this kind of export as "dark matter" that makes the current account figures look far worse than they really are.

Even if there are doubts about the existence of such economic dark matter, the current arrangement of deficit financing should be thought of as a codependency relationship between the United States and countries that rely on external triggers for economic growth. Changing the current system of financing the trade deficit will hurt these countries far more than it will hurt the United States. East Asian central banks are using their dollar purchases as a means of keeping their currencies undervalued to fuel export-led growth. For these governments, the costs of increased dollar holdings that fall in value relative to the euro pale next to the gains from pursuing status quo policies. The exchange-rate policies of many developing economies are acting as de facto development programs that assist in the integration of a massive pool of underemployed labor into the global economy. China alone has 200 million workers that need to be brought into the formal workplace. It could take up to two decades before their integration is complete. The current system can be thought of as a sequel to the old Bretton Woods arrangements that reintegrated Western Europe and Japan into the global marketplace. Even though the demise of Bretton Woods was inevitable, that system lasted close to twenty-five years; the current arrangements may last longer than the conventional wisdom believes.

There are also valid reasons to be skeptical about the possibility of the dollar's losing its status as the world's reserve currency. For that to happen, there must be a viable candidate to replace the dollar. The yuan, for obvious reasons, is not it. The yen—thought to be a rival to the dollar fifteen years ago—is a nonstarter. That leaves the euro. That currency has done a better job of maintaining its relative value in recent years, but the failure of the EU constitutional project, the collapse of the growth and stability pact designed to ensure fiscal responsibility, and acrimony over the EU budget have adversely harmed the euro in the short run. Over the long run, greater demographic vitality and a widening gap in productivity levels will ensure that the U.S. economy will outperform the eurozone—making dollar assets an attractive source for private investors.

Finally, even if some central banks are interceding to prop up the dollar, not all central banks are acting in that manner. The steady decline of the dollar against the euro in 2004 is one sign that equilibrating market effects are in play. The fall in the euro due to the rejection of the EU constitution is merely a temporary blip in what should be a continued dollar depreciation. The possibility of a dramatic fall in the dollar is unlikely, precisely because so many central banks are holding such large dollar reserves. They have an incentive to protect their investment and avoid capital portfolio losses. That would imply that any devaluation should be gradual enough to avoid a drastic macroeconomic shock.

CONCLUSION

There is no magic bullet to solve the ballooning trade deficit—indeed, the issue has less to do with trade policy than with macroeconomic policies at home and central bank interventions abroad.

The growing trade deficit does, however, demonstrate the integral political and economic links between trade policy and macroeconomic policy. The more the latter is unbalanced, the more difficult it becomes to pursue a free trade policy. Even if there is only a minimal economic connection between trade policy and the trade deficit, opponents of trade expansion will make a political connection between the two. The constraint on trade expansion will prove even more binding if the dollar experiences a hard landing and foreign central banks are designated as the obvious scapegoats. In recent simulations conducted by IMF economists, rising protectionism worsens the fallout from any fall in the dollar's value. Guiding the trade deficit down from existing levels will be necessary for Congress to ratify any future trade agreements.

WHITE PAPER B: THE INTERSECTION OF TRADE AND REGULATION

WHY REGULATION AFFECTS TRADE

Domestic regulation has been enmeshed with trade since the early 1990s. Negotiations within GATT and its successor, the WTO, have shifted much of the focus away from tariff reduction to ensuring that disparities in national regulations do not interfere with international trade. That happened in large part because GATT and the WTO succeeded in reducing border-level trade restrictions. For most areas of merchandise trade (excluding agricultural, textile, and clothing products), tariffs and quotas have been at low levels since completion of the Uruguay round of negotiations in 1994. Measures such as the Technical Barriers to Trade (TBT) agreement (negotiated during the Tokyo round) and the Sanitary and Phytosanitary (SPS) agreements (negotiated during the Uruguay round) have tried to reconcile the principles of national treatment and most-favored-nation (MFN) status with the different regulatory structures that exist in different countries.[4]

Regulatory issues have also appeared in the WTO dispute-settlement process and in the Doha round of negotiations. The effectiveness of the dispute-settlement process to adjudicate trade disputes has encouraged both the United States and the European Union to take long-standing disagreements to the WTO on issues ranging from defense subsidies to genetically modified

---

[4]National treatment is the idea that once an imported good enters a country, it is subject to the exact same treatment as domestically produced goods with regard to taxation, regulation, and distribution. Granting MFN status to a trading partner guarantees that partner the same trade concessions that are extended to other trading partners, and vice versa.

(GM) foods. Having a WTO panel decide disputes with such enormous ramifications poses risks and costs to all concerned parties. Many of the current transatlantic trade disputes expose deep philosophical conflicts over the proper way for government to regulate a market economy. For example, in the late eighties the European Union banned imports of American beef that had been treated with growth hormones. The United States brought a case to the WTO arguing that the EU ban unfairly discriminated against American exports. The WTO panel sided with the United States, ruling that the EU's food safety regulations did not rely on a scientific proof of harm (which would have been justified), but rather seemed designed to block U.S. imports. The European Union bowed to domestic public opinion, however, and refused to recognize the WTO panel's ruling. That entitled the United States to retaliate by sanctioning some EU products—but the beef ban remains in effect. We will likely see a replay of this outcome with genetically modified foods.

As these EU-U.S. conflicts demonstrate, on many of these issues the losing economic superpower is unlikely to accept the WTO ruling if it requires changing its domestic rules and regulations. Persistent noncompliance with WTO rulings by any of the major trading states undercuts the legitimacy and effectiveness of the WTO process in the eyes of all participating actors, making it difficult to use the WTO as a platform for advancing U.S. trading interests.

In the next several years, new regulatory concerns will become inextricably linked with the politics and policy of trade. Services such as finance and software represent an ever-increasing share of trade flows, and in time goods and services in sectors such as education, health care, and the law will become tradable. Trade negotiators will naturally shift their focus to these sectors as well. Services like these had never before been thought of as tradable goods, so they have no tariffs or quotas blocking foreign imports. Yet these sectors do have extensive domestic regulations that act as effective barriers to international exchange. Because most of these regulations were originally devised for domestic audiences, these policies will be far more difficult than tariffs or quotas to reconcile with international agreements. A contributing factor to the density of regulatory barriers is that many of the services that can be traded—airline transportation, education, telecommunications, utilities—have traditionally been run by state-owned enterprises. The domestic political cost of changing these regulations will be formidable; those with a vested interest in the status quo will lobby fiercely against any proposed change. The emergence of a broad coalition of civil-society groups hostile to trade only compounds the problem.

TRADE AND REGULATION: THE RADICAL CRITIQUE

Labor, consumer health, and environmental movements have become increasingly skeptical about the merits of further trade expansion. The extreme version of their critique is that economic liberalization fosters an unavoidable "race to the bottom" in regulatory standards around the world. According to this logic, the removal of trade and investment restrictions frees multinational corporations to scour the globe for the production location where they can earn the highest rate of return. National policies such as the strict protection of unions or rigorous health inspections or stringent environmental regulation ostensibly lower profits by raising the costs of production. Firms will therefore engage in "regulatory arbitrage," moving to countries with lax labor standards and low wage levels. Fearing a loss of their tax base and a rise in unemployment, countries have little choice but to lower their own standards to entice foreign investment and avoid capital flight.

The role of GATT and WTO in facilitating liberalization has further alienated these groups from the prospect of future trade expansion. The GATT/WTO regime has issued rulings against

U.S. environmental laws such as the Clean Air Act and the Marine Mammal Protection Act. That occurred most prominently in the so-called tuna/dolphin case, in which a 1991 GATT panel ruled that U.S. regulations requiring tuna fishermen to employ dolphin-safe nets discriminated against foreign fishermen. Antiglobalization activists have argued that these cases represent an international trade bureaucracy run amok.

The validity of these claims can be challenged on several grounds. There is little evidence to support the allegation that we are witnessing a race to the bottom in labor or environmental standards. The research arms of multiple international organizations—the Organization for Economic Cooperation and Development (OECD), the International Labor Organization (ILO), and the World Bank—have investigated claims that trade liberalization reduces regulatory standards and found no support for the proposition. Academic analyses have reached the same conclusion. Indeed, if anything, there is a positive relationship among trade flows, foreign direct investment, and effective regulation. Because the largest consumer markets are in the developed world, the stringent regulations in those countries often become the de facto standard for producers elsewhere.

As for the claim that the WTO is countermanding U.S. regulations, a closer look reveals a deeper truth. In the past decade, the WTO has demonstrated an increasing willingness to accept domestic rules and regulations to protect the environment as consistent with WTO obligations, provided that they are implemented in a way that does not discriminate against foreign producers. The WTO rulings that provoked the ire of activist groups were due to the U.S. government's application of these laws in ways that contravene international legal procedures. The federal government was forced to act in that manner because of lawsuits brought by NGOs in domestic courts.

TRADE, LABOR, AND THE ENVIRONMENT: THE MODERATE CRITIQUE

There are civil-society groups that reject the radical version of the antiglobalization critique—indeed, many of these groups favor trade liberalization. These groups also support greater environmental protections, and they point out the flaws of the current WTO regime. They argue that the WTO establishes an unfair playing field when balancing economic interests with other societal concerns, and that this imbalance needs to be corrected. The obvious comparison that these groups make is the contrast between the role of intellectual property rights and the role of labor and environmental standards in the WTO.

A major achievement of the Uruguay round was the Agreement on Trade-Related Aspects of Intellectual Property Rights (TRIPS). The TRIPS agreement incorporated and augmented the preexisting international agreements designed to protect copyrights, trademarks, patents, and industrial designs; increased the stringency of those standards; and added a much more rigorous enforcement regime to back up the agreement.

Until TRIPS, a clear line separated what the global trade rules covered from what they did not. The trade rules were designed to liberalize border-level barriers to the exchange of products, such as tariffs. Except for extreme circumstances (such as the use of prison labor), those rules said nothing about the processes for making products. TRIPS, however, was expressly designed to regulate production processes—namely, whether firms respected intellectual property rights in their operations. For the first time, the WTO regime affected domestic business regulation.

In contrast, efforts to push labor, environmental, and health concerns onto the WTO agenda have been less successful. The 1996 ministerial meetings in Singapore discussed whether the enforcement of core labor standards should be integrated into WTO decision-making. The ministerial declaration that year said no, instead reaffirming that the "ILO ... is the competent body to set and deal with these standards." The only affirmative action was a commitment for the secretariats of the WTO and the ILO to "continue their existing collaboration." A recent consultative board report for the WTO's director-general candidly described the extent of cooperation between the two bodies as "loose."

A slightly more encouraging story can be told with regard to trade and the environment. As previously discussed, the WTO dispute panels have not been unsympathetic to environmentalists' aims. A discussion of environmental protection was explicit in the Uruguay round. More recently, the WTO has extended an olive branch to various international environmental organizations. The European Union wanted a thorough discussion of trade-related environmental issues included in the Doha round. Environmental groups have proven to be more receptive than labor unions to the idea of trade liberalization through the WTO.

The case of GM foods, however, suggests the conflictual relationship that often exists between trade, consumer health, and environmental organizations. On food issues, the WTO's SPS Agreement explicitly defers to the Codex Alimentarus Commission, a joint Food and Agriculture Organization (FAO)-World Health Organization (WHO) body established in 1963 to establish appropriate safety standards, guidelines, and practices for the food trade. The Codex in turn argues that scientists have produced no significant evidence to suggest that GM foods harm either humans or the environment. In contrast, the Cartagena Protocol on Biosafety, an outgrowth of the 1992 Rio Convention on Biodiversity, endorses the "precautionary principle" in the treatment of large modified organisms. This principle states that potentially dangerous activities can be restricted or prohibited before they are scientifically proven to cause serious damage. The result is a potential legal stalemate, with the biosafety protocol's precautionary principle flatly contradicting the trade regime's norm of scientific proof of harm. Legal and development experts agree that it will be difficult to reconcile the WTO and Cartagena regimes, with environmental and trade groups on opposite sides of the political fence.

Another perceived difference between the treatment of trade-related IPR and other regulatory concerns has been the extent of access from concerned groups to WTO officials and meetings. In terms of access, multinational corporations are perceived to be able to interact with WTO participants on a more regular basis than are NGOs. Firms concentrated in the pharmaceutical, entertainment, and software sectors were the primary advocates of the TRIPS regime. Their success in shaping U.S. positions on IPR prior to the Uruguay round has been well documented. The demands by civil-society groups for a more open WTO, by contrast, have met only partial success. On the one hand, there has been a dramatic increase in the extent of NGO participation in the WTO ministerial meetings—an eightfold increase over eight years. On the other hand, member governments have been reluctant to make their negotiations too transparent to civil-society groups. The sensitive political nature of trade negotiations makes many member governments reluctant to allow information to become public too early.

ARE INTELLECTUAL PROPERTY RIGHTS DIFFERENT?

There are economic rationales for the disparity of treatment of intellectual property and social regulations in the trade regime. The absence of enforceable IPR across borders amounts to a nontariff barrier on trade in value-added goods. The ability of individuals in other countries to procure American innovations without paying for patent or trademark protection functions as an illegal subsidy for domestic producers. The negative effect of weak IPR enforcement is global in scale; reduced incentives for firms to invest in costly research and development also have a negative economic effect. There is abundant evidence to substantiate these claims—economists have shown that weak IPR enforcement is one factor that reduces foreign direct investment inflows, for example. The proposed remedies for this problem within the WTO system—trade sanctions—create incentives for governments to ratchet up their IPR enforcement.

The economic case for embedding labor and environmental regulations under the WTO rubric is less clear. Although the absence of environmental and labor standards can be thought of as an illegal subsidy for domestic producers, the evidence for such a claim is much weaker. There are negative side effects of lax environmental protection that clearly cross borders, but the same is not necessarily true with regard to labor standards (numerous studies conclude that the overwhelming bulk of labor abuses occur in production oriented toward domestic consumption, not trade-related consumption). Most importantly, the WTO remedies for the infraction of trade rules would not necessarily help the problem. For example, applying trade sanctions against countries that exploit child labor would force these children to work in the underground economy, where conditions are even worse.

Recommending against trade sanctions does not mean that steps to improve environmental protection and human rights cannot be encouraged. In the short run, the international institutional machinery designed to handle social problems is much weaker than the institutions designed to handle trade-related matters. Urging the creation of a new global environmental organization to coordinate the enforcement of existing environmental treaties need not conflict with the trade agenda. Augmenting the powers and technical assistance budget of the ILO also does not automatically require a confrontation with the WTO. The United States has recently cut back its contributions to these kinds of organizations; funneling more resources to these multilateral agencies would partially address this moderate critique.

In the long run, the best way to ensure that countries respect labor and environmental standards is to increase their national incomes and reduce poverty—in other words, by increasing rather than reducing trade. Income levels affect how citizens and governments choose between stringent regulations and economic growth. When the broad mass of society is concerned with acquiring the basic necessities of life, strict regulatory standards will be perceived as expensive luxury goods. Stringent regulations impose higher opportunity costs, since the investments needed to implement and monitor compliance with such regulations will hinder economic growth. However, as the broad mass of society acquires middle-class levels of income, social regulation begins to look more affordable. Therefore, as a country's median level of income increases, societal preferences for government regulation will shift in favor of more stringent standards.

Although there is an economic argument for differential treatment, the political argument runs in the other direction. Until the Uruguay round, the GATT regime clearly distinguished between the accepted practice of imposing product standards on traded goods and the discouraged practice of imposing restrictions on production processes. Most WTO members have argued that if the global trade body tried to regulate production processes, it would constitute an unwarranted intervention into the national regulations of member countries. Civil-society groups point out that this distinction is meaningless when determining the cause of environmental abuses.

The TRIPS regime violates this rule by expressly regulating processes of domestic production. The agreement also imposed a significant burden on developing countries to adhere to more rigorous standards. More recently, the agreement's effect on the provision of antiretroviral (ARV) drugs to treat AIDS threatened to polarize the global politics of trade. Pharmaceutical companies insisted that the U.S. government prevent the global spread of generically produced drugs that combat AIDS, increasing the price of patented drugs in many developing countries. Developing countries, acting in concert with U.S.-based NGOs, have argued that the emergency created by AIDS provides a justifiable public-health exception to the TRIPS regime. The ensuing wrangles between developed and developing economies have led to odd outcomes and publicly discomfiting U.S. positions at the negotiating table. For example, in 2003, the United States proposed to restrict the public-health flexibility of TRIPS to a minimal number of epidemic diseases—ignoring the potential for new pandemics. This position isolated the United States in these negotiations. At the same time, this policy debate prompted antiglobalization activists to make outlandish claims about the WTO's responsibility for the deaths of millions of Africans, when poverty and corruption are the true culprits. Whatever the valid reasons for linking IPR to trade, the negative political effects of TRIPS have been substantial.

TRADE AND REGULATION IN SERVICES

Some of the regulatory impediments in newly tradable sectors do not intersect with the interests of labor or environmental organizations. However, many of them do impinge on consumer health and safety matters that will trigger resistance from civil-society groups. For example, U.S.-based airlines are increasingly outsourcing routine aircraft maintenance checks to operations centers in other countries. In 2003, the inspector-general of the Department of Transportation (DOT) issued a report stating that the oversight of foreign contractors by the Federal Aviation Administration (FAA) was insufficient. Yet there is little evidence that outsourcing compromises airline safety, and the United States benefits from foreign airlines that outsource complex maintenance tasks to U.S. service centers. Nonetheless, media reports on the phenomenon have prompted consumer groups to complain.

Domestic opposition will likely grow as negotiations over services lead to questions about how to cope with the migration of service workers. At present, developing countries are pushing for greater liberalization in the trade of Mode 4 services, which is when the person performing a service crosses a border to do his or her job. U.S. businesses benefit greatly from these services, yet the homeland security measures taken since the terrorist attacks of September 11, 2001, function as an implicit tax on importers and exporters.

According to one estimate, U.S. companies lost more than $30 billion between July 2002 and March 2004 due to increased delays and denials in the processing of business visas. Microsoft Chairman Bill Gates warned in early 2005 that visa restrictions were limiting U.S. access to highly trained computer engineers from other countries, undercutting America's ability to innovate.

Despite the economic advantages of liberalizing Mode 4 services, such a move raises politically sensitive questions. The most obvious concern would be the effect that this kind of liberalization would have on U.S. immigration policies.

Opponents of increased immigration will claim that any liberalization of trade in Mode 4 services is a form of backdoor immigration. Another obvious concern would be whether terrorist groups could exploit any increase in the mobility of service workers to enter the United States. Finally, health scares such as the 2003 severe acute respiratory syndrome (SARS) crisis and more recent fears of an avian flu pandemic demonstrate how the movement of individuals and livestock can facilitate the spread of disease, making Mode 4 liberalization unpopular among consumer health and safety groups. Clearly, it will be difficult for the United States to show flexibility on this front.

Even the bargaining process for coping with the liberalization in service regulations will prove more difficult. The voluntary nature of the WTO negotiations for liberalization in services has slowed trade expansion on this front.[5] Another difficulty in future negotiations will be in coordinating different government bureaucracies and regulatory agencies. In the United States, the interagency process of establishing bargaining positions for trade talks will become more difficult as regulatory agencies are dragged into unfamiliar international negotiating forums.

---

[5]See White Paper D for more information.

THE RESISTANCE FROM THE DEVELOPING WORLD

Countries in the developing world oppose most forms of regulatory harmonization. On issues such as labor and environmental standards, the governments in these nations view American and European demands as a form of protectionism. For many of these countries, their comparative advantage in international trade is low-wage labor. However, if low wages are deemed to violate labor standards, then developing-country exports will suffer. The push by American unions to block the granting of TPA by Congress to the executive branch fuels these fears.

In negotiating on regulatory matters with the developing countries, the United States finds itself in an awkward position at times. At present, the United States has not ratified ILO conventions or environmental treaties that are considered relevant to advancing regulatory harmonization. Even if the United States complies with the spirit of many of these international agreements, the failure to accept these treaties provides other countries with useful diplomatic cover. Why should they adopt more rigorous social protections, they ask, if the United States refuses to sign international standards on the same issues?

A final complaint affects both social regulations as well as matters such as IPR or antitrust policy. The proper implementation of global regulations can cost upward of $100 million per country. Although this expense might seem trivial to the developed world, it can represent a significant fraction of developing-country budgets. Many of these countries lack the resources to properly train and fund the requisite agencies that would be necessary to enforce added regulatory burdens. Their experience in enforcing the TRIPS regime reinforces these concerns; even for middle-income developing countries, the cost of IPR enforcement has been more taxing than previously expected.

POLICY OPTIONS

There is a trade-off between advancing regulatory harmonization strictly as a means to advance the trade agenda or doing so as a means to export U.S. preferences on labor, environmental, and consumer health and safety standards. Reaching agreement on trade-related regulations is more difficult than reaching agreements on tariff reductions. For some countries, the inclusion of regulatory questions in the WTO agenda is a nonstarter; for some civil-society groups, the nonstarter is pursuing trade expansion without addressing regulatory safeguards.

One option is for the United States to tighten the linkage between access to American markets and compliance with American regulatory standards by ensuring that imported goods are manufactured in a manner congruent with American values. These concerns are best addressed in the WTO. There is precedent for such a move; Article XX of GATT, for example, expressly allows countries to ban imports made with prison labor. A push to have core labor standards and minimal levels of environmental protection considered within the WTO framework would, at a minimum, signal the seriousness of the U.S. position on these issues. Furthermore, repeated polling in the United States suggests that consumers will pay more for imported goods if those products are made in countries that meet minimum labor and environmental standards (although consumption patterns suggest that this preference is not strongly held).

The chances that WTO members will agree to incorporate these concerns are slim. A second-best option would be to propose a tighter link between rigorous regulatory standards and the Generalized System of Preferences (GSP) that the United States grants to developing-country members of the WTO. The GSP program waives all duties and tariffs for 4,000 products from 140 developing countries. Since 1984, the United States has linked GSP considerations to whether eligible countries adhere to "internationally recognized" worker rights—and some evidence suggests that the linkage has helped improve labor rights in the developing world. Yet GSP considerations have not been linked to environmental standards, and even on labor rights, private-sector groups complain of lax enforcement. Ratcheting up this instrument of statecraft would help to accelerate developing-country efforts on the regulatory front.

A policy complement to this strategy would be a reciprocity-based approach to the liberalization of trade in services. The growth of offshore outsourcing means that several important trading partners, such as China and India, now earn significant export revenues from their trade in services with the United States. A fair trade orientation would recommend that such practices be subjected to new forms of taxation unless these countries demonstrate a greater willingness to liberalize trade in higher value-added services—including air travel, finance, and telecommunications.

This reciprocity-based approach would need to address the political problem posed by the perception of unequal treatment of regulatory standards within the WTO. Threatening unilateral sanctions would generate antagonism in the developing world. As previously observed, incorporating civil-society concerns into the WTO regime will be very difficult. Indeed, President Bill Clinton's suggestion that the WTO consider trade sanctions for infractions of labor standards stymied the 1999 WTO ministerial meeting in Seattle.

An alternative inducement-based approach would use the carrot rather than the stick to push for improved regulation. The inclusion of labor and environmental agreements in bilateral or regional free trade agreements is one way to handle the regulatory question. Demands for improved labor conditions or environmental protection linked to political and economic benefits that come with an FTA are more politically palatable for the countries in question. Furthermore, the United States has enhanced bargaining leverage in an FTA situation. An increased number of FTAs would also generate progress on these issues.

Another carrot that could be bolstered within the WTO framework is the Standards and Trade Development Facility (STDF). This program was launched in 2002 to provide technical assistance to governments of developing countries for enforcing international SPS standards. The STDF is a joint creation of the FAO, the World Organization for Animal Health, the World Bank, the WHO, and the WTO. At present, the STDF is badly underfunded: the grants it provides amount to less than a million dollars. The STDF also covers only the SPS agreement from the Uruguay round. More robust funding and expanded mission aims (i.e., including labor standards and ILO participation) would alleviate a critical complaint by developing-country governments when regulatory matters are raised: that governments of developing countries lack the resources and the expertise to properly enforce labor, environmental, or IPR regulations.

The United States could similarly propose expanding the mandate of the Integrated Framework for Trade-Related Technical Assistance (IF) to the least-developed countries to include training national regulators on regulatory issues. The IF is a joint program of the WTO, IMF, World Bank, United Nations Conference on Trade and Development (UNCTAD), United Nations Development Programme (UNDP), and the International Trade Center. Such a move would be consistent with the IF's mandate to mainstream trade into national development agendas. It would also be consistent with calls from some NGOs to expand "aid-for-trade" opportunities—in which aid is provided to expand trade opportunities for the least-developed economies.

Rather than linking trade directly to regulatory issues, the United States could instead pursue trade expansion and regulatory arrangements on separate but complementary tracks. There is a strong argument to be made that trade sanctions will generate meager results on regulation. Even if sanctions generate some concessions in the short term, they eventually breed more resentment than they are worth. The threat to sanction Brazil or South Africa over pharmaceutical patents, for example, created such a backlash that the United States had to reverse course. In the long term, the best way to improve regulatory arrangements in the developing world is to accelerate their economic growth—which is best accomplished through trade expansion. In the short term, augmenting global governance structures beyond the WTO is the best way to address concerns about social regulation.

Such a "trade-plus" approach would prefer bolstering the ILO and creating a multilateral environmental organization to adding these issues to the WTO bailiwick. To do it properly, however, these organizations need to have sufficient resources for offering powerful inducements—rather than sanctions—to a wide swath of countries. The success of the WTO dispute-resolution mechanism has caused many to assume that trade sanctions are the most powerful tool of economic statecraft, and therefore, strong international agreements should have sanctions as their principal means of enforcement. Trade sanctions are the existing enforcement option for many multilateral environmental agreements, as well as the ILO. This approach argues that sanctions merely act to restrict trade even more than the original infraction of trade law. An approach that used monetary rewards and fines instead of trade sanctions would be more economically efficient and provide more precise incentives for compliance. However, for this system to work, the organizations must have resources commensurate with their assigned tasks.

Finally, this approach recognizes that the important actors in the liberalization of services are the United States and the European Union. As measured by aggregate market size, the economies of the United States and the European Union were both more than $11.5 trillion at the end of 2004. The American and European shares of global merchandise trade are more than twice that of any other WTO participant; their share of the global services trade is even larger. When their market size is combined, the United States and the European Union are responsible for roughly 40 percent of global output, 41 percent of world imports, 59 percent of inward foreign direct investment, 78 percent of outward foreign direct investment, and 88 percent of global mergers and acquisitions. If these two entities can agree on regulatory harmonization, it will be easier to achieve a global agreement.

Both the United States and the European Union have brought many regulatory disputes to the WTO dispute-settlement mechanism for resolution. It is questionable whether the dispute panels are the best institution to address these issues. While these panels and the Appellate Body are undoubtedly aware of political considerations in issuing their rulings, the legal rationales for decision-making make it difficult to craft political compromises.

Because of the numerous regulatory disputes between the two parties—ranging from data privacy to GM foods to tax rules—the "trade-plus" approach would recommend the creation of a Regulatory Impediments Initiative (RII) between the United States and the European Union. This strategy would be akin to the Structural Impediments Initiative (SII) launched between Japan and the United States more than a decade ago. Such a forum would consist of multiple negotiation tracks; beyond the government-to-government channel, this initiative could encompass the revival of the Transatlantic Business Dialogue (TABD), as well as a Transatlantic Social Dialogue (TSD) between civil-society groups.

The RII would not solve the regulatory disputes that plague the transatlantic relationship—indeed, many of them may not have an immediate resolution. Yet combining these issues into a forum outside the WTO would serve several purposes. First, it would delay the decision by either party to lodge a formal complaint within the WTO. The United States and the European Union would benefit from having the opportunity to craft a compromise rather than risking a WTO arbitration ruling that could hurt both parties. Bilateral talks permit the kind of give-and-take in bargaining that a WTO panel bound by legal norms cannot provide. Second, the bringing together of multiple regulatory questions would allow for the possibility of cross-issue trade-offs. Historically, this approach has proven successful in trade talks with the European Union during the nineties. Third, an RII forum would encourage all sides to tamp down their rhetoric. Public clashes between American and European trade officials create political uncertainty about the future course of trade negotiations, needlessly roiling global markets.

CONCLUSION

Future trade liberalization will affect two categories of domestic regulation that will inspire resistance from two separate but equally problematic audiences. For civil-society groups suspicious of the benefits of globalization, the chief concern is that trade liberalization will reduce the stringent U.S. regulations governing the treatment of labor, the environment, and consumer health and safety. For service sectors and professional guilds wary of import competition, the chief concern is that trade liberalization will alter the arcane set of rules and regulations that govern their professional lives. Politically, these sectors will have a strong tactical incentive to mobilize civil-society groups as a way to protect their livelihood. A proper program of trade expansion will need to address these regulatory concerns one way or another.

WHITE PAPER C: DISTRIBUTING THE GAINS FROM TRADE

Winners and Losers

Trade is a win-win arrangement between countries. However, it is not always a win-win arrangement within a country's borders. One economist recently estimated that for every dollar created through trade expansion, another five dollars are redistributed within the economy between winners and losers. That leads to several policy questions: Who wins from trade expansion? Who is made worse off? To what extent should the losers be compensated for the effects of trade expansion? Who should provide the compensation, and how?

The answer to the first question is relatively simple. Standard trade models suggest that as a group, America's low-skilled workers bear the greatest costs from trade expansion. The United States does not have a comparative advantage in sectors that use significant amounts of low-skilled labor. Naturally, trade expansion will hurt low-skilled workers and their families. Cheaper goods will partially compensate for these losses—but not entirely.

The Losses from Freer Trade

The costs of trade take three specific forms, all of which matter for a fair trade orientation. First, job losses from import competition and offshore outsourcing, although not as significant as suggested in the media, nevertheless exist. As former Federal Reserve Chairman Alan Greenspan observed in 2004,

Even in the best of circumstances, discharged workers experience some loss of income in a transition to a new job and the associated new skills. Indeed, finding a new job takes time, and typically results in at least a temporary drop in pay. That loss, especially in a soft labor market, is not only a short-term drag on aggregate incomes but also a source of stress on the affected individuals.

The numbers confirm Greenspan's assessment. Recent studies have found that the reemployment rate for workers displaced by import competition ranges between 60 and 65 percent, and the average reemployment earnings range between 13 and 17 percent lower.

The second and related effect is an increase in economic uncertainty among low-skilled workers. The job churn that comes from a globally integrated American economy reduces expectations of job stability. The percentage of workers who lose their jobs because of import competition or offshore outsourcing may be small, but the percentage of workers who know someone who has lost his or her job because of trade is much larger. In this sense, public perceptions about trade are akin to perceptions about crime: knowing a victim of crime makes the problem often appear to be greater than it actually is. Although such fears may be exaggerated, the economic effects of these fears are very real. Economic uncertainty creates a mind-set among low-income families that shortens their time horizons when mapping out their purchasing choices. This psychological effect prevents these workers from making rational investments for the future.

The final effect of trade expansion comes through a decline in relative wages. Reduced demand for low-skilled labor in the import-competing sectors decreases overall domestic demand for unskilled labor. When demand declines, so do wages. This phenomenon affects low-skilled workers in both tradable and nontradable sectors. This negative effect has the widest range, in that unskilled workers working in a purely domestic sector still experience a small negative shock from trade expansion.

Technological innovation has caused a new category of workers to be harmed by international trade. Innovation has helped standardize and segment what used to be complex job skills into more simple tasks. This phenomenon decreases the demand for high-skilled workers in some sectors such as information-technology support and business-process management. The spread of the Internet has further facilitated the outsourcing of these tasks to locations outside the United States. Although innovations have created jobs in newer fields such as nanotechnology, the churn nevertheless has had costs. The increase in economic uncertainty that comes with these innovations is at the heart of worsening public attitudes toward trade expansion. Even if technological innovation is the underlying cause for this job churn, trade is seen as the proximate cause.

HOW IMPORTANT ARE TRADE EFFECTS?

Trade's contribution to unemployment, job churn, and lower wages is undeniably real, but free trade economists would nevertheless argue that the magnitude of the trade effect can be exaggerated. Trade has often been articulated as the primary cause for the slow growth in wages for the past three decades. Statistical analysis suggests that trade plays a minimal role in any explanation of this phenomenon. For example, in 1998, the Council of Economic Advisers concluded that trade was responsible for at most 10 to 15 percent of the increase in wage inequality during the 1980s. Recent scholarship goes further, pointing out that when alternative explanations—such as technological innovation and investments in education—are factored into the equation, trade is found to have almost nothing to do with the slow increase in average compensation.

The increase in the job churn from trade expansion is also open to question, as figures 4a and 4b demonstrate. If trade is the primary cause of increased job turnover, then offshore outsourcing

Figure 4a. Mass Layoffs Due to Trade

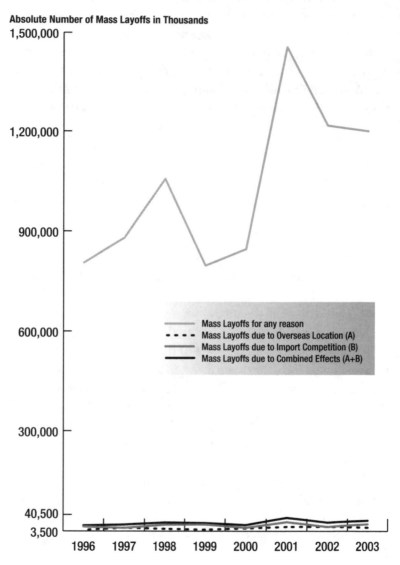

Source: Bureau of Labor Statistics; see http://data.bls.gov/labjava/outside.jsp?survey=ml.

Figure 4b. % of Mass Layoffs Due to Trade

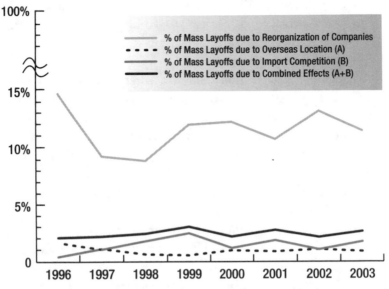

Source: Bureau of Labor Statistics; see http://data.bls.gov/labjava/outside.jsp?survey=ml.

should have triggered explosive growth in the gross number of jobs destroyed in the U.S. economy. Yet between 2001 and 2002, the aggregate number of total jobs lost in the U.S. economy fell by 9.6 percent. Between 2001 and 2004, the Bureau of Labor Statistics (BLS) record of total nonfarm layoffs and discharges showed a downward rather than an upward trend. Neither of these trends is consistent with the hypothesis that trade integration increases job destruction. If trade is increasing the turnover in jobs, the effect is not particularly powerful.

A similar story can be told with regard to job losses from trade: they are smaller than job losses from other factors. For example, the BLS estimated that in the first quarter of 2004, 4,633 workers were laid off en masse because of offshore outsourcing. In January 2004, Kodak announced a mass layoff of 15,000 workers—not because of outsourcing, but because the explosive growth of digital photography had reduced demand for film. The percentage of mass layoffs due to either import competition or offshore outsourcing has held steady at less than 5 percent for the last several years. To be sure, the BLS figures, by focusing only on mass layoffs, undercount the total number of jobs lost through offshore outsourcing. Nevertheless, this example demonstrates the relative importance of nontrade factors in contributing to job losses.

That kind of exaggeration points to a larger problem in discussing the distributional effects of trade. Although an open American economy creates new winners and losers, other factors have much greater distributional effects. In the short term, macroeconomic policy has a greater impact on growth, employment, and wages than does trade policy. In the long term, the pace and fallout of technological innovation also has a much greater impact than trade has on the economy.

Addressing the distributional effects of trade expansion does serve a useful political purpose. Providing some compensation to those who are hurt because of trade expansion is more in keeping with the economic principle of trade expansion as a win-win move and helps to improve the political environment surrounding trade liberalization. A 2004 survey by GMFUS found that the following statement generated 71 percent approval among Americans, and roughly equal support from trade optimists and trade pessimists:

> International trade has both positive and negative effects. International trade brings a lot of benefits—lower consumer prices, more choice—but also causes a lot of disruption in millions of workers' households with people losing their jobs. With the world becoming a smaller and smaller place, we need to make trade work for everyone. For us here in the United States and Europe, that means we need to invest more in skills and technology so that our economy becomes more flexible and innovative—that is where our best opportunities lie for the future.

This logic echoes statements made by Greenspan on coping with the global economy:

> Americans have not been obsessed with the distribution of income but have instead placed much greater emphasis on the need to provide equality of opportunity. But equal opportunity requires equal access to knowledge. We cannot expect everyone to be equally skilled. But we need to pursue equality of opportunity to ensure that our economic system works at maximum efficiency and is perceived as just in its distribution of rewards.

In any discussion about compensation for the costs of trade, the unspoken question is whether social insurance policies should be directed toward the economy as a whole or tailored to compensate the individuals directly affected by trade expansion. The United States is unique among the developed economies because it has insurance policies that directly target workers who lose their jobs due to foreign competition. Should there be better compensation programs for workers displaced by trade than for workers who lose their jobs for other reasons?

On at least one level, the answer is yes. The American public views economic losses from trade in a different way than it views economic losses from other causes. For example, technological innovation is not politically stigmatized for destroying as well as creating jobs. Trade liberalization, however, bears that stigma. For Americans, losing one's job because of American ingenuity is one thing; losing one's job because of foreign competition is another thing entirely. From an economic perspective, discussing social insurance due to trade losses would appear to be a low-level priority. Yet from a political perspective, such policies are necessary in order to make trade expansion a viable policy option.

TRADE ADJUSTMENT ASSISTANCE

The primary program to compensate those who suffer from exposure to the global economy is the TAA program. TAA has been in existence in one form or another since it was introduced in the 1962 Trade Expansion Act. From 1981 to 2001, workers were eligible for TAA when they could demonstrate that import competition was responsible for their having been laid off. In return for actively participating in a job search or retraining, TAA recipients were entitled to receive one year of cash assistance (beyond standard unemployment insurance), two years of retraining, and supplemental allowances for job searches and relocation.

The TAA Reform Act of 2002 added significant new benefits to the TAA program, as Table 5 demonstrates. In addition to expanding the eligibility requirements, the duration of monetary assistance was lengthened, protection of health coverage was added, and Alternative Trade Adjustment Assistance (ATAA)—a wage insurance program for workers aged 50 or older—was added.

Table 5: Changes in Trade Adjustment Assistance

TAA feature	1981–2001	2002 TAA Reform Act
Eligibility	Workers demonstrating that increased imports or increased competition "contributed importantly" to layoffs and decline in production	Criteria expanded to include farmers as well as upstream and downstream workers displaced by plant relocations
Requirements for receipt of benefits	Active participation in job search and authorized training	Secretary of Labor given greater autonomy in waiving requirements
Duration of cash assistance	52 weeks	78 weeks
Health coverage	None	Tax credit for 65 percent of health care premiums
Wage insurance	Demonstration program (never implemented by states)	ATAA: 50 percent of differential between old and new salaries (capped at $10,000)

POLICY OPTIONS

The different policy orientations offer contrasting approaches to deal with the distribution of gains from trade: a fair trade orientation stresses that even if TAA were fully funded, the end result would still be dislocation at the household level for many Americans. The best way to reduce such dislocations is to ensure they happen only when U.S. firms do not have a comparative advantage on a level playing field. If foreign producers are displacing American workers because of predatory pricing strategies or state subsidies, then the psychic and financial costs of dislocation outweigh the temporary gains from trade. To address this problem, the fair trade approach would recommend a muscular use of the antidumping and countervailing duty provisions in U.S. trade law to prevent unnecessary churn in the domestic economy.

Another fair trade recommendation would be to provide greater warning to workers who are displaced by offshore outsourcing. When firms plan to outsource as few as fifteen jobs from the United States, they should be required to notify the affected workers three months in advance of implementation. Such a requirement would not halt offshore outsourcing, but it would serve a useful purpose. Advance notification requires firms to factor in the public-relations costs of their outsourcing decisions. Forcing firms to consider this cost will, at a minimum, slow the pace of offshore outsourcing.

A free trade orientation recognizes the utility of TAA in two ways: as a means to ensure broader political support for trade liberalization, and as a means to make trade more akin to a win–win scenario for all Americans. The evidence suggests that the retraining option has enabled more TAA-supported workers to find jobs than workers who have not received training. Although TAA has been in place for more than thirty years and was reformed only four years ago, public-opinion polling suggests that the current arrangement fails to address worker anxiety. The options for reform range from small to large.

One omission in the current TAA program is that its coverage is skewed toward the manufacturing sector. Historically, it made sense because, until recently, manufacturing accounted for the overwhelming bulk of imports that competed with domestic production. However, the standardization and segmentation of some service activities, combined with the spread of the Internet, has increased the trade of services. Although the Labor Department ruled in April 2006 that software programmers could now be covered by TAA, that ruling was designed not to apply to other service sector workers. TAA should apply to the entire spectrum of traded goods and services, not only to manufactured goods.

Another way TAA could alleviate worker anxiety would be for the federal government to advertise the way TAA increases the portability of health care coverage. A Gallup survey taken in 2004 demonstrated that workers feared the loss of health care and other benefits far more than they feared the losses of their jobs from import competition. The 2002 reforms introduced a refundable and advanceable tax credit that could be used toward the purchase of up to 65 percent of health care coverage. However, for this tax credit to kick in, recipients must exhaust conventional unemployment insurance. Many workers therefore lose their health insurance prior to receiving the tax credit that is intended to allow them to keep their coverage. Efforts to publicize, expand, and accelerate receipt of this benefit would help to reduce worker anxieties.

A related question is the extent to which the different provisions of the TAA program are implemented by the executive branch. Some agencies have outperformed others by a wide margin. For example, interviews with trade-affected workers suggest that the Internal Revenue Service has vigorously executed the health care tax credit portion of TAA. At the same time, there have been complaints that the Labor Department has been more sluggish in administering and advertising the ATAA portion of TAA. The Labor Department's opacity in promulgating the criteria for TAA and ATAA eligibility after the 2002 reforms has also been a sticking point in implementation. The Labor Department waited until the day of implementation to issue guidance to state governments in charge of administering the programs. The Government Accountability Office (GAO) reports that the Labor Department has insufficiently advertised the TAA program to potential recipients, which helps to explain the small number of applicants in recent years. Between August 2003 and December 2004, only 1,403 workers received ATAA; common sense suggests that more workers should have received the benefit. Ensuring an equality and transparency of effort from the different agencies of the executive branch would help to improve both the performance and the perceptions regarding the existing TAA program.

Addressing the wage effects from trade poses more interesting policy trade-offs. At the governmental level, programs like ATAA could be expanded to include workers under the age of fifty. Yet the ATAA program as currently formulated has a peculiar incentive scheme. Because the program is capped after $50,000, individual workers ostensibly receiving the benefit are taxed at a 100 percent rate for any wage earned above that level—even if the new wage is significantly lower than the old one. This is a small problem if only low-wage workers are affected by import competition; it becomes a bigger problem if more job categories are affected.

The wage insurance option, however, remains an attractive one because it is the one compensation program that increases the financial incentive for displaced workers to find new jobs. It may be appropriate to augment the ATAA program by offering tax incentives for the private sector to provide wage insurance schemes for employees. One recent study by the McKinsey Global Institute estimates that such schemes could be created for as little as four to five cents for each dollar accrued to a firm from the benefits of trade expansion. Firms that face public-relations problems from offshore outsourcing are already taking steps in that direction. IBM, for example, received considerable negative publicity from leaked memos indicating that it was planning on firing 3,000 workers and outsourcing their positions overseas. To counter that publicity— and to boost employee morale—the firm announced the creation of a two-year, $25 million retraining fund for its employees who fear job losses from outsourcing.

Finally, to achieve liberalization in politically sensitive sectors such as agriculture, it would be useful to provide monetary cushions to those interests most harmed by increased imports. Currently, the barriers for agricultural firms to qualify for TAA are high: producers must demonstrate a 20 percent drop in price caused by imports over five years. The rewards are capped at $10,000. Not surprisingly, few agricultural producers receive TAA. To blunt opposition to future trade liberalization, agricultural interests must find it easier and more rewarding to receive compensation. Because many agribusiness owners are quite wealthy—sugar plantation owners, to name one example—this step could look bad politically. Yet from a free trade perspective, offering lucrative benefits in the short term to liberalize the most protected sectors makes sense.

It is also possible to advocate a free trade orientation while maintaining a more jaundiced view of certain aspects of the TAA program. Although TAA can move trade expansion closer to a win-win arrangement, questions can be raised regarding the extent to which these kinds of insurance policies should be implemented—or should be prioritized for trade-affected workers. Economic analyses of unemployment insurance programs demonstrate that when the monetary benefits or duration of those programs increase, so does the average duration of unemployment for affected workers. Increasing the duration of unemployment can have debilitating effects on earning potential; one study found that a 10 percent increase in the length of unemployment reduces the post-unemployment wage by 1 percent. Another study compared the pre-2002 TAA program to other unemployment insurance programs and found that the added benefits of TAA had no effect on post-unemployment wages. More generally, trade insurance programs can distort the market signals that differences in wages and employment stability are supposed to send.

It is a distinct possibility that the government would receive greater returns on policies that maximize economic growth and employment than on policies that specifically target trade-displaced workers. During the 1990s, the implementation of NAFTA and the Uruguay round of trade negotiations undeniably increased the number of jobs lost due to import competition. The economic boom of that decade, however, generated so many new job opportunities that the trade-related employment losses looked trivial by comparison.

This approach would therefore recommend a series of growth policies designed to capitalize on the opportunities generated from a more open global economy. Prudent macroeconomic policies, low tax burdens, business-friendly immigration policies, and a greater willingness to fund public goods for emerging sectors would be the obvious steps to take. The higher the rate of economic growth, the less concern there will be about income redistribution.

The funding of basic research and education would be particularly useful in boosting growth. At present Japan and South Korea spend more on R&D as a percentage of GDP than the United States. Although public spending on R&D is scheduled to increase in the United States, government funds are concentrated in defense and homeland security. Those sectors are undeniably important, but the focus on them has caused funding levels for all other R&D programs to be flat or declining. Basic research funded by the government complements applied R&D funded by the private sector. The more that the U.S. government spends on basic research and higher education, the greater the incentive private firms will have to invest in innovative activities. Ensuring robust research programs in leading-edge sectors would promote greater innovation, as well as ensure that American universities and colleges remain centers of comparative research excellence. Your plan to double spending in the federal agencies that support basic research programs in the physical sciences and engineering—as part of your Competitiveness Initiative—is a good first step in this direction.

CONCLUSION

Trade disproportionately harms low-wage workers and the tradable sectors that employ them. While trade expansion can increase both unemployment and job turnover, and lower wages, its effect should not be exaggerated; compared to the effects of other macroeconomic shocks, trade's effects are small. The existing TAA program is a good first step toward addressing the distribution questions, but other policy reforms are available to ensure that trade expansion can be a win-win arrangement for all Americans.

WHITE PAPER D: THE MULTIPLE TRACKS OF TRADE DIPLOMACY

A BRIEF HISTORY

In recent decades, the United States has pursued trade expansion through multilateral, regional, bilateral, and unilateral tracks. Since World War II, the United States has made a multilateral trade agenda its top priority. The United States was the undisputed leader in launching the modern trading system. The initial rounds of GATT eliminated many quantitative restrictions and established MFN status—the principle that any trade concessions extended to one signatory must be extended to all signatories. The other important concept behind GATT was national treatment—the idea that once an imported good enters a country, it is subject to the exact same treatment as domestically produced goods with regard to taxation, regulation, and distribution.

These two nondiscriminatory principles are at the core of the multilateral trade agenda. In the five and a half decades since GATT was signed, successive rounds of negotiations led to drastic reductions in tariffs, the curtailment of nontariff barriers, and the creation of the WTO and its dispute-resolution process for adjudicating trade conflicts.

These multilateral efforts have yielded significant achievements. In 1947, the average tariff rate was approximately 40 percent of a traded good's value; at the start of the Doha round of WTO negotiations that figure was less than 4 percent. The WTO's dispute-resolution system has decided more cases in the first eight years of its existence than the GATT system handled over its fifty-year life span. The United States has been a big winner from the dispute-resolution process, winning concessions in more than 60 percent of the complaints it has initiated. The GATT/WTO regime has presided over a massive increase in merchandise trade over the past half-century.

U.S. interest in bilateral and regional trade agreements is comparatively more recent. The United States reached its first bilateral free trade agreement with Israel in 1985. The Canada-U.S. Free Trade Agreement (CUSTA) was approved in 1988. The first regional trade agreement came with the passage of NAFTA in 1993. Pledges soon followed to complete a Free Trade Area of the Americas by 2005 and to liberalize trade among the members of the Asia-Pacific Economic Cooperation (APEC) forum by 2020. More recently, the Central American Free Trade Agreement was ratified in the summer of 2005, and regional FTAs have been proposed with southern Africa and the greater Middle East. In the past five years, the number of bilateral FTAs has dramatically increased, with the United States reaching agreements with Jordan, Chile, Singapore, Australia, Morocco, Bahrain, Oman, and Peru. The National Association of Manufacturers estimates that nearly half of all U.S. exports go to FTA partners.

Before World War II, the United States relied on unilateral measures to advance its trading interests. Although the tariff has receded as a policy tool, the United States still has several unilateral instruments available to it: Section 301 of U.S. trade law permits the USTR to threaten and implement sanctions against countries that restrict U.S. exports. To deal with foreign firms that receive government subsidies or price their wares below market prices, the United States can assess countervailing and antidumping duties on the relevant goods. On the regulatory side, the United States has a number of sector-specific laws that can ban foreign imports from countries that violate regulatory standards. The International Emergency Economic Powers Act (IEEPA) empowers the president to employ economic sanctions against any country perceived to be a threat to national security (although that measure has never been used to advance the trade agenda). Many of these unilateral policy options appear designed to reduce trade flows, but the most obvious unilateral move to advance free trade is to reduce U.S. barriers to imports from other countries. The African Growth and Opportunity Act (AGOA) is one example of this phenomenon.

ARE THE NEGOTIATION TRACKS COMPLEMENTARY?

Prioritizing one negotiation track over another implies a trade-off between the different approaches, although there does not always have to be a trade-off. The U.S. government has successfully used unilateral, bilateral, and regional trade diplomacy as bargaining tactics to convince other parties of its willingness to walk away from the negotiation table unless it received certain concessions. When the Uruguay round of GATT talks bogged down, the Reagan and first Bush administrations devoted greater attention to regional deals with Canada and Mexico and escalated the use of unilateral measures such as Section 301. These threats proved useful in steering the Uruguay round toward an outcome that benefited American interests.

Regional and bilateral FTAs spur action on the multilateral front only when the proposed FTAs represent a credible example of substantial trade benefits for the United States. CUSTA and NAFTA were credible because the large market size and geographic proximity of Canada and Mexico made them natural trading partners with the United States. At this juncture, only the FTAA would generate a comparable level of credibility for the United States vis-à-vis other WTO participants—and these negotiations are currently bogged down. Beyond the FTAA, it would be difficult to describe the existing regional and multilateral tracks of trade negotiations as complementary. The relationship between the unilateral and multilateral tracks is similar.

THE ADVANTAGES OF THE MULTILATERAL TRACK

The advantages of focusing U.S. efforts on trade liberalization through the WTO are considerable. First and foremost are the economic benefits that come from liberalization under the WTO rubric. Because all of the major trading states are members of the WTO, the benefits from liberalization in that context would be considerable. In contrast, the effects of trade liberalization with countries targeted for bilateral FTAs are anticipated to be small. Many of the other candidate FTA countries on the list, such as the United Arab Emirates, would have a minimal effect on the American economy.

The WTO's enhanced dispute-resolution process is another reason to push for liberalization in the multilateral venue. In contrast to the old GATT regime—in which any member country, including those involved in the trade dispute, could veto any recommended enforcement action—the current dispute-resolution process has greater autonomy in authorizing punishment for violating countries. The creation of the Appellate Body provides a useful layer of review that increases legitimacy for and confidence in the institution. The relative speed with which the dispute-resolution panels can issue decisions is another advantage of the WTO process. The efficiency of the process has improved to the point where a high percentage of cases are completed without appeal. In its first decade of existence, the WTO process has reviewed more than 325 complaints, a much higher rate than in the GATT era.

The enhanced dispute-resolution process, the expertise of WTO officials, and the accumulation of legal precedents generated from panel rulings has endowed the WTO with significant legal authority over trade matters. Statistical analyses of American trade disputes reveal that a favorable WTO panel ruling vastly increases the likelihood that a trading partner will make the desired concessions. That is true regardless of whether trade sanctions are threatened inside or outside the WTO process. In terms of the major U.S. trading partners, this finding holds with particular force with regard to Japan. (Panel rulings have had less impact on the European Union.) The ability of the WTO to ensure national compliance with trade rules and regulations has been of considerable benefit to the United States. The progress that has been made in getting other countries to enforce IPR would not have taken place without the backing of the WTO.

The WTO's legitimacy among foreign governments will prove to be useful as the organization continues to tackle trade-related issues beyond the scope of tariffs and quotas. There are a number of barriers pertaining to trade policy that the WTO is only beginning to tackle: trade in financial services, procurement regulations, investment-related issues, and the movement of service professionals across borders. All of these issues affect industries in which the United States possesses a comparative advantage, and thus further progress on these fronts would be a boon for the American economy.

Finally, there are two foreign policy motivations for pushing greater trade liberalization through the WTO process. The first is to correct the perception—deserved or not—of the United States as a "rogue superpower" since the September 11, 2001, terrorist attacks. For the United States, the WTO represents the ideal type of multilateralism: an institution run by member governments that promotes clearly articulated norms and the vigorous enforcement of those norms. It is in the U.S. national interest to reward those international organizations that best reflect these American principles.

The second political reason is to send the necessary signal to non-WTO members about the value of membership. Although the WTO currently has 148 members, many countries have yet to be granted membership. These governments include the Russian Federation, Vietnam, Ukraine, Iran, Serbia, Libya, and Kazakhstan. U.S. interests with regard to all of these countries would be better served with a greater respect for the rule of law. At the present moment, all of these countries have signaled a willingness to make significant concessions for WTO admission. If the United States were to deemphasize its paramount commitment to the organization, these countries would be less likely to take steps toward promoting the rule of law.

The Drawbacks of Multilateralism

The WTO-first option also has significant drawbacks. The most obvious problem is the rising transaction costs of each WTO round of negotiations. As Table 6 indicates, over the past forty years each successive round of GATT/WTO trade talks has taken longer to complete. The Uruguay round took seven years from start to finish—and during that time, NAFTA was proposed, negotiated, and ratified. The Uruguay agreement produced 26,000 pages of treaties, codicils, and national agreements. After five years, Doha is at a standstill.

There are three significant reasons for the growing difficulties with WTO negotiations. The first is the robust increase in the number of WTO signatory parties. It is simply easier to get 13 states to agree on anything than it is to get 148 to do the same. At a minimum, the costs of communication have dramatically increased.

More importantly, the number of actively participating countries has increased. Up to and including the Uruguay round, the chief negotiating parties in the GATT/WTO process were the so-called Quad—the United States, the European Community, Japan, and Canada. In theory, GATT operated on a consensus-

Table 6: GATT/WTO Negotiation Rounds

Name of round	Years of negotiation	Number of participants
Geneva	1947	23
Annecy	1949	13
Torquay	1950	38
Geneva	1956	26
Dillon	1960–61	26
Kennedy	1964–67	62
Tokyo	1973–79	102
Uruguay	1986–94	123
Doha	2001–	149

based decision-making system. In fact, when the Quad reached agreement, its consensus was dictated to the rest of the world.

In the Doha round, however, China, India, and Brazil created their own negotiating bloc. African countries exercised their voice as well. These new players helped to sabotage the Cancun ministerial meeting in the fall of 2003. There are several reasons to believe that this bloc of developing countries will impose serious constraints on advancing American interests within the WTO. The sheer number of developing countries gives them effective veto power in any international organization that operates by consensus. The larger developing countries have much greater market power than they did thirty years ago, and these economies all have dramatically higher growth rates than the United States, making it impossible to ignore their negotiating positions. The outcome of the Uruguay round has also made these countries wary about agreeing to further concessions. Although the developed world was able to create an IPR regime that began operating immediately after the Uruguay round was ratified, the concessions on agriculture and textiles were back-loaded and are only now being implemented.

These countries are also wary about the resource implications of compliance with new WTO obligations. Developed countries have proposed that WTO rules should be extended to cover investment, procurement, and antitrust policy. As with IPR, these issues actually require an expansion of government regulation and supervision of economic activity. While liberalization on these fronts will generate long-run gains for all participating countries, there are short-term costs for governments in the developing world. Even for large developing countries, the opportunity costs of training and staffing competent bureaucracies on arcane regulations is formidable.

Liberalizing the exchange of services—an important goal for the United States—will also pose problems for the WTO. As previously discussed in White Paper B of this report, the ability to trade in services such as telecommunications, finance, construction, education, and business processing is a comparatively recent phenomenon. The barriers to exchange in these areas do not take the traditional form of tariffs; they appear more commonly as domestic regulations. Altering domestic regulations carries greater political costs than do tariff reductions. Developing countries also see little incentive in liberalizing these sectors, because the United States and the European Union possess an overwhelming comparative advantage in many of these services (although the rise of offshore outsourcing may create such an incentive).

The negotiating structure of the General Agreement on Trade in Services (GATS) also makes liberalization in this arena less likely. Because the bottom-up, voluntary scheduling of GATS concessions by WTO members allows governments to set their own schedule for liberalization without any preset timetable, the pace of liberalization has lagged. In the Doha round's first four years, more than forty countries did not make any offer to open up their markets to foreign service providers. Furthermore, the procedural format of the talks—a series of bilateral requests and offers between service exporters and importers—acts as an additional brake on progress. The service talks use a "negative-list" approach to liberalization, in which national sectors are considered closed to foreign competition unless the government proposes them for liberalization. This format generates less liberalization than "positive-list" approaches, in which protected sectors are the exception rather than the rule.

The final cost of the WTO approach is the domestic political effort required for its success. While presidential TPA is useful for regional and bilateral trade negotiations, it is absolutely essential to move forward in the WTO. Securing this authority produced a difficult floor fight in Congress the last time it came up in 2001 and 2002. Public attitudes toward trade expansion have soured since then. Once the authority expires in 2007, reauthorization will be another uphill climb.

The Advantages of Regional and Bilateral Approaches

There are strong arguments in favor of the regional and bilateral approaches. It is worth remembering that although global trade liberalization took place via the multilateral route in the twentieth century, liberalization happened through the bilateral route in the nineteenth century. The 1860 Cobden-Chevalier Treaty between the United Kingdom and France triggered a cascade effect among the governments of that era. Other governments, concerned with being left out of the benefits from that treaty, signed bilateral trade deals containing MFN clauses. The result was a reinforcing process of competitive liberalization, as each country secured preferential access with the major trading states. That process provided the foundation for the open global economy in the late 1800s. A case can be made that a similar process is under way today, as the United States, Japan, and China try to catch up to the European Union's plethora of regional and bilateral trade accords.

One way the current era differs from the nineteenth century is the absence of an MFN clause in modern preferential trade agreements. That slows but does not stop the current process of liberalization. The political economy of trade diversion still generates competitive incentives for a growth in FTAs. Producer groups in the United States that lose out because of trade diversion to other countries participating in FTAs will actively lobby for the United States to sign additional FTAs—which can be negotiated more quickly than a WTO round. For a concrete example, Canada implemented an FTA with Costa Rica in 2003, obtaining from Costa Rica an expanding zero-tariff quota that permits an increasing number of frozen french fries to enter Costa Rica from Canada duty-free. At the same time, pre-CAFTA U.S. tariffs on Costa Rican frozen fries remained at the WTO bound rate of 40 percent. That led U.S. potato growers and processors to advocate forcefully for the CAFTA negotiations as a way to restore their competitive balance vis-à-vis Canada.

Bilateral and regional trade agreements also afford the United States much greater bargaining power than the WTO process.

Within the WTO, the European Union possesses comparable economic size and bargaining power. The norm of consensus decision-making acts as another constraint on U.S. influence. The countries targeted for FTAs with the United States are all much smaller. For these countries, guaranteeing preferential access to the American market is a significant achievement. They are therefore more willing to accede to American requests during the negotiation process. It gives the United States an opportunity to expand trade beyond goods to include services and investment—a process that would prove more difficult in the WTO. For example, recent FTAs carry more stringent protections for IPR than currently exist in the TRIPS regime.

There are additional political reasons to pursue the regional and bilateral track. The power asymmetry vis-à-vis candidate FTA countries allows the United States to pursue noneconomic aims as well. For example, recent FTAs have included arrangements or accords to enforce labor and environmental standards, promote anticorruption policies, and encourage democratization. Some critics have argued that these arrangements are merely window dressing, but academic studies suggest that the agreements can have an appreciable impact on the policy choices of our FTA partners. Noneconomic aspects of FTAs have also made it easier to ensure congressional ratification. At the same time, the prospect of a preferential trading arrangement with the United States is a powerful reward for loyal allies.

The aforementioned significance of regulation as a residual barrier to trade provides another incentive for regional and bilateral trade diplomacy. For the most part, the European Union prefers more stringent regulatory standards when it comes to production processes. This stringency has been reflected in trade issues ranging from GM foods to data privacy. Each preferential trading agreement the European Union signs is another means through which it can expand its regulatory bloc. One way for the United States to ensure that its own regulatory standards remain viable and visible in the global economy is to expand its number of FTA partners.

THE DRAWBACKS OF REGIONALISM AND BILATERALISM

The economic and political disadvantages to pursuing the regional and bilateral route must be acknowledged. Beyond the FTAA, the direct economic advantages from the proposed list of FTAs are small. Table 7 lists the candidate FTA countries and where they rank in terms of their volume of trade with the United States. The economic gain from successful liberalization via the WTO process would be much greater than the combined effect from these

Table 7: Candidate FTA Countries and Their Volume of Trade with the United States

Agreement	Country	Trade Volume with United States ($ Million)	Rank	Percent of Total U.S. Trade
Bilateral FTA	Malaysia	44,154	10	1.715
	Panama	2,496	64	0.097
	South Korea	71,450	7	2.775
	Thailand	27,126	19	1.053
	United Arab Emirates	9,946	35	0.386
Andean FTA	Colombia	14,261	31	0.554
	Ecuador	7,738	45	0.300
FTAA	Antigua & Barbuda	194	134	0.008
	Argentina	8,672	43	0.337
	Bahamas	2,469	65	0.096
	Barbados	425	110	0.016
	Belize	315	121	0.012
	Bolivia	512	104	0.020
	Brazil	39,782	14	1.545
	Dominica	65	166	0.003
	Grenada	88	159	0.003
	Guyana	295	122	0.011
	Haiti	1,135	85	0.044
	Jamaica	2,078	67	0.080
	Paraguay	947	91	0.037
	Saint Kitts & Nevis	144	146	0.006
	Saint Lucia	167	140	0.006
	Saint Vincent & Grenadines	61	167	0.002
	Suriname	409	111	0.016
	Trinidad & Tobago	9,320	39	0.362
	Uruguay	1,087	87	0.042
	Venezuela	40,373	13	1.568
SACU FTA	Botswana	246	128	0.010
	Lesotho	408	112	0.016
	Namibia	243	129	0.009
	South Africa	9,747	36	0.378
	Swaziland	211	131	0.008

FTAs. A proper FTAA would be a significant gain, but the current status of FTAA negotiations makes this desired outcome highly unlikely. Brazilian resistance to the original goal of a binding FTAA with wide scope has converted the aim of the negotiations into a much less ambitious "FTAA lite." Under the new arrangement, FTAA members can choose to opt in or out of various parts of the agreement, putting a damper on hemispheric integration.

Another drawback of the regional and bilateral approach is that the United States is far behind the European Union on this track of negotiations. The European Union has actively pursued a regional and bilateral agenda for the past decade. As of 2005, the European Union had signed some kind of preferential trading agreement with all but nine trading partners (Australia, Canada, Hong Kong, Japan, New Zealand, Singapore, South Korea, Taiwan, and the United States). American FTAs are much more comprehensive than European trade agreements; nevertheless, the United States has significant ground to make up in order to be on a par with the European Union.

It could be argued that the race for FTAs will achieve an open trading system by other means. Indeed, the American pursuit of such deals has spurred other countries—such as Japan and China—to begin to pursue such negotiations. However, none of these proposed FTAs has the MFN principle embedded within them. Therefore, in contrast to the previous era of globalization, genuine trade expansion can take place only if every country in the world signs an FTA with every other country. Because of the fears of losing out from trade diversion, most developing countries with small markets will still have an incentive to negotiate such deals. Nevertheless, the regulatory and noneconomic structures that are contained in modern FTAs will impose significant delays on this outcome.

The likely outcome of allowing the unchecked proliferation of preferential trading agreements would be a world in which most countries would have some form of FTA with the major trading powers—the European Union, the United States, Japan, and

China. These agreements, however, would likely be riddled with more exceptions than a standard WTO round would permit. It is doubtful that any of the major trading states would have preferential trading agreements with one another. It is likely that such a regime would retard trade liberalization between developing countries. Economic analyses conclude that the global economic benefits from such a scenario are smaller by several orders of magnitude than the benefits to be achieved by completion of the Doha round.

The regional and bilateral approach also poses a threat to the integrity and future of the WTO. The proliferation of FTAs undermines the nondiscriminatory MFN principle that is at the core of the WTO. GATT's Article XXIV does permit the creation of FTAs or customs unions that liberalize trade beyond WTO arrangements. The current understanding of Article XXIV in the original GATT is that "the purpose of such agreements should be to facilitate trade between the constituent territories and not to raise barriers to the trade of other Members with such territories; and that in their formation or enlargement the parties to them should to the greatest possible extent avoid creating adverse effects on the trade of other Members." Because many FTAs generate added regulatory burdens on outside parties, and because FTAs can generate as much trade diversion as trade creation, there are legal grounds for WTO members to lodge a complaint challenging one of these FTAs.

A related problem with the regional and bilateral approach is the political signal it sends. If the United States indicates that it will bestow more attention on reaching FTAs than on restoring the Doha round and planning for further liberalization in the WTO, then other countries will lose faith in the multilateral track of negotiations. In early 2005, a WTO consultative report concluded that "the 'spaghetti bowl' of customs unions, common markets, regional and bilateral free trade areas, preferences, and an endless assortment of miscellaneous trade deals has almost reached the point where MFN treatment is exceptional treatment. . . . [T]he term might now be better defined as LFN, Least Favored Nation Treatment." A decline in respect for the WTO would have calamitous consequences for American trade policy. The rigor of the dispute-resolution mechanism and the past rounds of successful tariff liberalization have netted significant economic benefits for the United States. Simply put, the United States has too much invested in the WTO simply to walk away from it.

THE ADVANTAGES OF UNILATERALISM

The advantages of the unilateral approach are simple and direct. The biggest plus of unilateralism is that when it works, the gains are tangible and the domestic political costs are minimal. The clout of the American economy commands so much influence that often the threat of trade sanctions is sufficient to cut through a diplomatic impasse. If the United States can wield its market power as a means of extracting trade concessions, then it can force other countries into lowering their trade barriers without having to make reciprocal concessions. When the threat of economic sanctions works, sanctions never need to be implemented because the United States can extract the trade concession it seeks short of taking action against the country in question. When used against countries that depend on the American export market, such a threat can generate improved access for U.S. exporters. In the past, the threat and implementation of unilateral economic sanctions has pushed countries to boost protection of IPR, respect the ocean environment, and demonstrate greater respect for labor unions.

The current moment offers the United States an excellent opportunity to exploit its unilateral option. Prior analyses show that when a country runs a sizable trade surplus with the United States, it is more likely to make substantive concessions in the face of economic pressure. Given the large trade surpluses that many countries currently run with the United States, more pressure may yield more liberalization.

Unilateral measures can also indirectly lead to progress on liberalization. The threat of sanctions forces other major trading states to recalculate the costs of delaying the Doha round of the WTO—just as the use of Section 301 in the late 1980s spurred progress in the Uruguay round. Unilaterally, the United States can also make liberalizing gestures that have little effect on the trade balance but serve foreign policy and development interests. For example, unilaterally reducing barriers to sub-Saharan African imports beyond the AGOA has little effect on aggregate trade flows but is seen as a symbol of American generosity toward an entire continent.

A final advantage of pursuing this route of trade diplomacy is that, compared to the multilateral and regional tracks, Congress is required to do very little. The only thing it must do is support the Super 301 process, which requires the USTR to issue an annual report on barriers to U.S. exports and establish specific timetables toward the elimination of such barriers. Super 301 authority lapsed in 2002 and requires congressional reauthorization. The sentiment underlying Super 301 resonates with an American public convinced that other countries are exploiting U.S. economic openness—making this approach an easy political sell. Although congressional resistance to the unilateral reduction of tariffs and quotas for African goods might be slightly greater, opposition would be more politically difficult if the move were framed as development policy rather than as a question of trade politics.

THE DRAWBACKS OF UNILATERALISM

The disadvantages of the unilateral approach are equally clear. Unilateral economic sanctions are of limited use against the very countries that would have the greatest impact on the U.S. exporting base. The European Union's market size is comparable to that of the United States—and the threat of sanctions has historically had little effect on the European Union's trade diplomacy. The repeated use of Section 301 against Japan has inured that country against the threat of sanctions. China's trade surplus with the United States provides some leverage, but China's geopolitical position renders it a very unlikely candidate to make concessions in the face of economic threats. This leaves very few significant trading countries to receive the brunt of U.S. economic pressure. A deeper problem with the unilateral approach is that, on its own, it is incapable of generating a great deal of trade expansion. At best, the unilateral approach can ensure that other countries live up to their obligations under the WTO and the GSP that the United States grants to developing-country members of the WTO. This approach can do little to force liberalization beyond that point.

Unilateralism can also lead to more market distortions rather than greater liberalization. Consider the case of auto imports from Japan in the early 1980s. The response to U.S. threats to restrict imports unilaterally was an agreement among Japanese auto producers to engage in voluntary export restraints (VERs). The VERs had a number of bad economic effects. They reduced price competition, making it more expensive for Americans to buy cars. They accelerated the ability of Japanese producers to catch up to their American counterparts, as Japanese producers shifted production from economy to luxury autos, cutting into U.S. manufacturers' profit margins more quickly than if VERs had not been imposed. In the end, there was only one group of net beneficiaries from the VER arrangement: Japanese auto producers.

Finally, the unilateral track would also jeopardize U.S. investments in the WTO framework. As with the bilateral and regional tracks, unilateral action undercuts the WTO's legitimacy and alters other countries' expectations about the WTO's value for the future. The foreign policy ramifications of repeatedly threatening countries with sanctions would also generate negative consequences in other arenas of foreign policy. Our failure to increase quotas for Pakistani textile exports during a critical phase of Operation Enduring Freedom in Afghanistan is but one example of the way that protectionism can negatively affect national security. Largesse in Africa would not offset the ill will that U.S. sanctions would threaten to create along the Pacific Rim.

CONCLUSION

The trade-offs among the multilateral, regional, bilateral, and unilateral approaches to trade are clear. The multilateral approach via the WTO would lead to drawn-out and difficult negotiations across a wide range of issues. Furthermore, significant political capital would have to be spent to ensure congressional support. Successful negotiations in the WTO format, however, would lock in significant economic benefits for the United States. The push for regional and bilateral FTAs would generate more immediate and tangible successes on the trade front. The noneconomic benefits from this approach—in the form of rewarding allies and advancing American regulatory concerns—would also be significant. Yet the economic impact of the regional and bilateral approach would be considerably less, and in the long run would threaten to undercut the hard-won gains achieved at the WTO. The unilateral approach potentially allows the United States to extract trade concessions without having to reciprocate in kind. The cost of this approach, however, subsumes the costs of the regional and bilateral approach and also raises larger foreign policy concerns.

FURTHER READING

GENERAL AND HISTORICAL BACKGROUND ON AMERICAN TRADE POLICY

Baldwin, David Allen. *Economic Statecraft*. Princeton: Princeton University Press, 1985.

Bayard, Thomas O., and Kimberly Ann Elliott. *Reciprocity and Retaliation in U.S. Trade Policy*. Washington, DC: Institute for International Economics, 1994.

Dam, Kenneth W. *The Rules of the Global Game: A New Look at U.S. International Economic Policymaking*. Chicago: University of Chicago Press, 2004.

Destler, I.M. *American Trade Politics*. 3rd ed. Washington, DC: Institute for International Economics, 1996.

Goldstein, Judith and Robert O. Keohane, eds. *Ideas, Interests, and American Trade Policy*. Ithaca: Cornell University Press, 1993.

Kunz, Diane B. *Butter and Guns: America's Cold War Economic Diplomacy*. New York: Free Press, 1997.

Spero, Joan E., and Jeffrey A. Hart. *The Politics of International Economic Relations*. 5th ed. New York: Routledge, 2001.

Zeiler, Thomas W. "Managing Protectionism: American Trade Policy in the Early Cold War." *Diplomatic History* 22 (July 1998): 337–60.

THE ECONOMIC EFFECTS OF TRADE LIBERALIZATION:

Bhagwati, Jagdish N. *In Defense of Globalization*. New York: Oxford University Press, 2004.

Bouët, Antoine, Simon Mevel, and David Orden. "Two Opportunities to Deliver on the Doha Development Pledge." International Food Policy Research Institute Research Brief no. 6, Washington, DC, July 2006.

Bradford, Scott C., Paul L.E. Grieco, and Gary Clyde Hufbauer. "The Payoff to America from Global Integration," in C. Fred Bergsten, ed., *The United States and the World Economy: Foreign Economic Policy for the Next Decade.* Washington, DC: Institute for International Economics, 2005.

Dollar, David, and Aart Kraay. "Spreading the Wealth." *Foreign Affairs* 81 (January/February 2002): 120–33.

Dorman, Peter. "The Free Trade Magic Act," Economic Policy Institute Briefing Paper no. 111, Washington, DC, September 2001.

Frankel, Jeffrey A., and David Romer. "Does Trade Cause Growth?" American Economic Review (June 1999): 379–99.

Groshen, Erica L., Bart Hobijn, and Margaret M. McConnell. "U.S. Jobs Gained and Lost Through Trade: A Net Measure." *Current Issues in Economics and Finance.* Federal Reserve Bank of New York, August 2005.

Helpman, Elhanan. *The Mystery of Economic Growth.* Cambridge: Belknap, 2004.

Irwin, Douglas A. *Free Trade under Fire.* Princeton: Princeton University Press, 2002.

Madrick, Jeff, "Questioning Free Trade Mathematics," *New York Times,* March 18, 2004.

Morici, Peter. *The Doha Round: No Help for America's Trade Deficit?* College Park, MD: University of Maryland, April 2006.

Polaski, Sandra. *Winners and Losers: Impact of the Doha Round on Developing Countries.* Washington, DC: Carnegie Endowment for International Peace, 2006.

Rangaswami, Viji. "Nickel and Diming the Poor: U.S. Implementation of the LDC Initiative." Carnegie Endowment for International Peace Policy Outlook no. 26, Washington, DC, July 2006.

Rodrik, Dani. *Has Globalization Gone Too Far?* Washington, DC: Institute for International Economics, 1997.

Scott, Robert E. "U.S.-China Trade, 1989–2003," Economic Policy Institute Working Paper no. 270, Washington, DC, January 2005.

Smith, Adam. *An Inquiry into the Nature and Causes of the Wealth of Nations.* 1776. Reprint, ed. Edwin Cannan, Chicago: University of Chicago Press, 1976.

Stiglitz, Joseph E., and Andrew Charlton. *Fair Trade for All: How Trade Can Promote Development.* New York: Oxford University Press, 2006.

Tonelson, Alan. *The Race to the Bottom: Why a Worldwide Worker Surplus and Uncontrolled Free Trade Are Sinking American Living Standards.* Boulder, CO: Westview Press, 2000.

Wolf, Martin. *Why Globalization Works.* New Haven: Yale University Press, 2004.

THE POLITICAL CAUSES AND EFFECTS OF TRADE LIBERALIZATION

Bacchus, James. *Trade and Freedom.* London: Cameron May Ltd., 2004.

Chua, Amy. *World on Fire: How Exporting Free Market Democracy Breeds Ethnic Hatred and Global Instability.* New York: Doubleday, 2002.

Drezner, Daniel W. "The Hidden Hand of Economic Coercion." *International Organization* 57 (Summer 2003): 643–59.

Esty, Daniel C., et al. *Working Papers: State Failure Task Force Report.* McLean, VA: Science Applications International Corporation, 1995.

———. *The State Failure Task Force Report: Phase II Findings.* McLean, VA: Science Applications International Corporation, 1998.

Gartzke, Erik. "Economic Freedom and Peace," in *Economic Freedom of the World: 2005 Annual Report.* Washington: Cato Institute, 2005.

Griswold, Daniel T. "Trading Tyranny for Freedom: How Open Markets Till the Soil for Democracy." Trade Policy Analysis no. 26, Center for Trade Policy Studies, Cato Institute, Washington, DC, January 6, 2004.

Hafner-Burton, Emilie. "Globalizing Human Rights? How Preferential Trade Agreements Shape Government Repression, 1972–2000." Ph.D. diss., University of Wisconsin, Madison, 2004.

Ikenberry, G. John. *After Victory.* Princeton: Princeton University Press, 2000.

Kant, Immanuel. "Perpetual Peace: A Philosophical Sketch," in H. S. Reiss, ed., *Kant: Political Writings.* New York: Cambridge University Press, 1970.

King, Gary, and Langche Zeng. "Improving Forecasts of State Failure." *World Politics* 53 (July 2001): 623–58.

McMillan, Susan M. "Interdependence and Conflict." *Mershon International Studies Review* 41 (May 1997): 33–58.

National Intelligence Council. *Mapping the Global Future: Report of the National Intelligence Council's 2020 Project,* available at http://www.cia.gov/nic/NIC_2020_project.html.

Nye, Joseph S. *The Paradox of American Power: Why the World's Only Superpower Can't Go It Alone.* New York: Oxford University Press, 2002.

Oneal, John R., and Bruce Russett. "The Kantian Peace: The Pacific Benefits of Democracy, Interdependence, and International Organizations, 1885–1992." *World Politics* 52 (October 1999): 1–37.

Paris, Roland. "Peacebuilding and the Limits of Liberal Internationalism." *International Security* 22 (Fall 1997): 54–89.

Pevehouse, Jon C. *Democracy from Above: Regional Organizations and Democratization.* New York: Cambridge University Press, 2005.

Wilson, Dominic, and Roopa Purushothaman. *Dreaming with BRICs: The Path to 2050.* Global Economics Paper no. 99, Goldman Sachs, New York, October 2003.

OFFSHORE OUTSOURCING

Bardham, Ashok Deo, and Cynthia Kroll. *The New Wave of Outsourcing.* Fisher Center for Real Estate and Urban Economics Report, University of California, Berkeley, Fall 2003.

Bhagwati, Jagdish, Arvind Panagariya, and T.N. Srinivasan. "The Muddles over Outsourcing." *Journal of Economic Perspectives* (Fall 2004): 93–114.

Blinder, Alan S., "Offshoring: The Next Industrial Revolution?" *Foreign Affairs* 85 (March/April 2006): 113-128.

Bronfenbrenner, Kate, and Stephanie Luce. "The Changing Nature of Corporate Global Restructuring: The Impact of Production Shifts on Jobs in the U.S., China, and Around the Globe." Report prepared for U.S.-China Economic and Security Review Commission, October 2004. Available at http://www.uscc.gov/researchpapers/2004/cornell_u_mass_report.pdf.

Drezner, Daniel W. "The Outsourcing Bogeyman." *Foreign Affairs* 83 (May/June 2004): 22–34.

Farrell, Diana, "U.S. Offshoring: Small Steps to Make It Win-Win." *The Economists' Voice* 3, 2006, available at http://www.bepress.com/ev/vol3/iss3/art6.

McKinsey Global Institute. *Offshoring: Is It a Win-Win Game?* San Francisco, CA, August 2003.

Samuelson, Paul A. "Where Ricardo and Mill Rebut and Confirm Arguments of Mainstream Economists Supporting Globalization." *Journal of Economic Perspectives* 18 (Summer 2004): 135–46.

Schultze, Charles L. *Offshoring, Import Competition, and the Jobless Recovery.* Policy Brief no. 136, Brookings Institution, Washington, DC, July 2004.

U.S. Government Accountability Office. *Current Government Data Provide Limited Insight into Offshoring of Services.* Washington, DC, September 2004.

AMERICAN PUBLIC OPINION AND TRADE LIBERALIZATION

Audley, John J., and Hans Anker. *Reconciling Trade and Poverty Reduction.* Washington, DC: German Marshall Fund of the United States, July 2004.

Bouton, Marshall M., and Benjamin I. Page. *The Foreign Policy Disconnect: What Americans Want from Our Leaders but Don't Get.* Chicago: University of Chicago Press, 2006.

Council on Foreign Relations and the Pew Research Center. *Foreign Policy Attitudes Now Driven by 9/11 and Iraq.* August 2004.

Drezner, Daniel W. "How to Market Trade in America," in Phoebe Griffith and Jack Thurston, eds., *Free and Fair: Making the Progressive Case for Removing Trade Barriers.* London: Foreign Policy Centre, 2004.

Herrmann, Richard K., Philip E. Tetlock, and Matthew N. Diascro. "How Americans Think about Trade: Reconciling Conflicts among Money, Power, and Principles." *International Studies Quarterly* 45 (March 2001): 191–218.

Kull, Steven, and I.M. Destler. *Misreading the Public: The Myth of a New Isolationism.* Washington, DC: Brookings Institution Press, 1999.

Kull, Steven. "Americans on Globalization, Trade and Farm Subsidies." Program on International Policy Attitudes, Washington, DC, January 2004.

Page, Benjamin I., and Jason Barabas. "Foreign Policy Gaps Between Citizens and Leaders." *International Studies Quarterly* 44 (September 2000): 355-76.

Rousseau, David L. "Motivations for Choice: The Salience of Relative Gains in International Politics." *Journal of Conflict Resolution* 46 (June 2002): 394–426.

Scheve, Kenneth F., and Matthew J. Slaughter. *Globalization and the Perceptions of American Workers.* Washington, DC: Institute for International Economics, 2001.

———. "Economic Insecurity and the Globalization of Production." *American Journal of Political Science* 48 (October 2004): 662–74.

POLITICAL AND LEGAL PROCEDURES FOR TRADE POLICY

Elliott, Kimberly Ann. "Preferences for Workers? Worker Rights and the US Generalized System of Preferences." Working Paper, Institute for International Economics, Washington, DC, May 2000, available at http://www.iie.com/publications/papers/paper. cfm?ResearchID=313.

Feenstra, Robert C., ed. *The Effects of U.S. Trade Protection and Promotion Policies.* Chicago: University of Chicago Press, 1997.

Ikenson, Daniel J. "Nonmarket Nonsense: U.S. Anti-Dumping Policy toward China." Trade Briefing Paper no. 22, Center for Trade Policy Studies, Cato Institute, Washington, DC, March 7, 2005.

Schott, Jeffrey J. *The Uruguay Round: An Assessment.* Washington, DC: Institute for International Economics, 1994.

Shapiro, Hal, and Lael Brainard. "Trade Promotion Authority Formerly Known as Fast Track: Building Common Ground on Trade Demands More Than a Name Change." *George Washington International Law Review* 35 (2003): 1–54.

Stoler, Andrew L. "Treatment of China as a Non-Market Economy." December 2003, available at http://www.iibel.adelaide.edu.au/docs/Shanghai%20Speech.pdf.

United States Trade Representative, *U.S. China Trade Relations: Entering a New Phase of Greater Accountability and Enforcement.* Washington, DC, February 2006.

REGIONAL AND BILATERAL VS. MULTILATERAL TRADE NEGOTIATIONS

Dam, Kenneth W. "Cordell Hull, the Reciprocal Trade Agreement Act, and the WTO." John M. Olin Law and Economics Working Paper no. 228, University of Chicago, October 2004.

Davis, Christina L. *Food Fights over Free Trade: How International Institutions Promote Agricultural Trade Liberalization.* Princeton: Princeton University Press, 2003.

Lazer, David. "The Free Trade Epidemic of the 1860s and Other Outbreaks of Economic Discrimination." *World Politics* 51 (July 1999): 447–83.

Mansfield, Edward L., and Helen V. Milner, eds. *The Political Economy of Regionalism.* New York: Columbia University Press, 1997.

Stein, Arthur. "The Hegemon's Dilemma: Great Britain, the United States, and the International Economic Order." *International Organization* 38 (Spring 1984): 355–86.

Sutherland, Peter, et al. *The Future of the WTO: Addressing Institutional Challenges in the New Millennium.* Geneva: World Trade Organization, 2004.

MACROECONOMIC POLICY AND THE TRADE DEFICIT

Bergsten, C. Fred, and John Williamson, eds. *Dollar Adjustment: How Far? Against What?* Washington, DC: Institute for International Economics, 2004.

Bernanke, Ben. "The Global Savings Glut and the U.S. Current Account Deficit." Homer Jones Lecture, St. Louis, MO, March 10, 2005.

Chinn, Menzie D. *Getting Serious about the Twin Deficits, A Council Special Report.* New York: Council on Foreign Relations Press, September 2005.

Dooley, Michael P., David Folkerts-Landau, and Peter Garber. "Direct Investment, Rising Real Wages, and the Absorption of Excess Labor in the Periphery." NBER Working Paper 10626, July 2004.

Goldstein, Morris. "Adjusting China's Exchange Rate Policies." Paper presented at the International Monetary Fund seminar on China's Foreign Exchange System, Dalian, China, May 26–27, 2004.

Hausmann, Ricardo and Federico Sturzenegger. "Global Imbalances or Bad Accounting? The Missing Dark Matter in the Wealth of Nations." Center for International Development Working Paper No. 124, Harvard University, Cambridge, MA, January 2006.

Higgins, Matthew, Thomas Klitgaard, and Cédric Tille. "The Income Implications of Rising U.S. International Liabilities," *Federal Reserve Bank of New York Current Issues in Economics and Finance* 11 (December 2005): 1–8.

Humpage, Owen F. "A Hitchhiker's Guide to the U.S. Current Account Problem." Federal Reserve Bank of Cleveland, October 2004.

Krugman, Paul R., and Maurice Obstfeld. *International Economics,* 5th ed. Boston: Addison-Wesley Longman, 1999.

Levy, David H., and Stuart S. Brown. "The Overstretch Myth." *Foreign Affairs* 84 (March/April 2005): 2–7.

Mann, Catherine L. *Is the U.S. Trade Deficit Sustainable?* Washington, DC: Institute for International Economics, 1999.

Quiggin, John. "The Unsustainability of U.S. Trade Deficits." *The Economists' Voice* 1, 2004, available at http://www.bepress.com/cgi/viewcontent.cgi?article=1020&context=ev.

Roubini, Nouriel, and Brad Setser. "The U.S. as a Net Debtor: The Sustainability of the U.S. External Imbalances." Working Paper, New York University, November 2004, available at http://pages.stern.nyu.edu/~nroubini/papers/Roubini-Setser-US-External-Imbalances.pdf.

TRADE AND REGULATION

Bhagwati, Jagdish N., and Robert E. Hudec, eds. *Fair Trade and Harmonization: Prerequisites for Free Trade?* Cambridge: MIT Press, 1996.

Braithwaite, John, and Peter Drahos. *Global Business Regulation.* Cambridge: Cambridge University Press, 2000.

Destler, I.M., and Peter J. Balint. *The New Politics of American Trade: Trade, Labor, and the Environment.* Washington, DC: Institute for International Economics, 1999.

Drezner, Daniel W. "Globalization at Work: Bottom Feeders." *Foreign Policy* 121 (November/December 2000): 64–70.

———. "Globalization and Policy Convergence." *International Studies Review* 3 (Spring 2001): 53–78.

———. *All Politics Is Global: Explaining International Regulatory Regimes.* Princeton: Princeton University Press, 2007.

Drucker, Peter F. "Trading Places." *The National Interest* 79 (Spring 2005): 101–107.

Elliott, Kimberly Ann, and Richard B. Freeman. *Can Labor Standards Improve under Globalization?* Washington, DC: Institute for International Economics, 2003.

Eskeland, Gunnar S., and Ann E. Harrison. "Moving to Greener Pastures? Multinationals and the Pollution-Haven Hypothesis." Policy Research Working Paper no. 1744, World Bank, Washington, DC, March 1997.

Esty, Daniel C. "Bridging the Trade-Environment Divide." *Journal of Economic Perspectives* 15 (Summer 2001): 113–30.

International Labor Organization. *Labour and Social Issues Relating to Export Processing Zones.* Geneva: ILO, 1998.

Klein, Naomi. *No Logo: Taking Aim at the Brand Bullies.* London: Picador, 2000.

Lewis, Jeffrey, and David Nixon. "Transnational Regulatory Conflict and the Problems of Deeper Integration." Paper presented at the annual meeting of the International Studies Association, Chicago, February 2001.

Maskus, Keith. "Regulatory Standards in the WTO." Working Paper no. 00-1, Institute for International Economics, January 2000. Available at http://www.iie.com/publications/wp/2000/00-1.htm.

Millstone, Erik, and Patrick van Zwanenberg. "Food and Agricultural Biotechnology Policy: How Much Autonomy Can Developing Countries Exercise?" *Development Policy Review* 21 (September 2003): 655–67.

Organization for Economic Cooperation and Development (OECD). *International Trade and Core Labour Standards.* Paris: OECD, 2000.

———. *Trade, Employment, and Labour Standards: A Study of Core Workers' Rights and International Trade.* Paris: OECD, 1996.

Prakash, Aseem, and Susan K. Sell. "Using Ideas Strategically: Examining the Contest Between Business and NGO Networks in Intellectual Property Rights." *International Studies Quarterly* 48 (January 2004): 143–75.

Quinlan, Joseph P. *Drifting Apart or Growing Together? The Primacy of the Transatlantic Economy.* Washington, DC: Center for Transatlantic Relations, 2003.

Sell, Susan K. *Power and Ideas: North-South Politics of Intellectual Property and Antitrust.* Albany: SUNY Press, 1998.

Slaughter, Anne-Marie. *A New World Order.* Princeton: Princeton University Press, 2004.

Thomas, Urs. P., et al. "The Biosafety Protocol: Regulatory Innovation and Emerging Trends." *Revue Suisse de Droit International et de Droit Européen* 10 (April 2000): 513–58.

Wheeler, David R. *Racing to the Bottom? Foreign Investment and Air Pollution in Developing Countries.* Policy Research Working Paper no. 2524, World Bank, Washington, DC, November 2000.

Winham, Gilbert R. "Regime Conflict in Trade and Environment: The Cartegena Protocol and the WTO." Paper presented at the annual meeting of the International Studies Association, Chicago, February 2001.

ALLOCATING THE BENEFITS OF FREE TRADE

Baicker, Katherine, and M. Marit Rehavi. "Policy Watch: Trade Adjustment Assistance." *Journal of Economic Perspectives* 18 (Spring 2004): 239–55.

Kletzer, Lori G., and Howard Rosen, "Easing the Adjustment Burden on U.S. Workers" in C. Fred Bergsten, ed., *The United States and the World Economy: Foreign Economic Policy for the Next Decade.* Washington, DC: Institute for International Economics, 2005.

Krugman, Paul, and Robert Z. Lawrence. "Trade, Jobs and Wages." *Scientific American* (April 1994).

Lafer, Gordon. *The Job Training Charade.* Ithaca: Cornell University Press, 2002.

Lawrence, Robert Z., and Matthew J. Slaughter. "International Trade and American Wages in the 1980s: Giant Sucking Sound or Small Hiccup?" *Brookings Papers on Economic Activity* 2 (1993): 161–211.

Lindsey, Brink. *Job Losses and Trade: A Reality Check.* Trade Briefing Paper no. 19, Cato Institute, Washington, DC, March 17, 2004.

Marcal, Leah E. "Does Trade Adjustment Assistance Help Trade-Displaced Workers?" *Contemporary Economic Policy* 19 (January 2001): 59–72.

Slaughter, Matthew J., and Philip Swagel. "The Effect of Globalization on Wages in the Advanced Economies." Staff Studies for the World Economic Outlook, International Monetary Fund, Washington, DC, December 1997.

Uchitelle, Louis. *The Disposable American: Layoffs and Their Consequences.* New York: Knopf, 2006.

BACKGROUND TABLES

Figure 5a. Free Trade Map

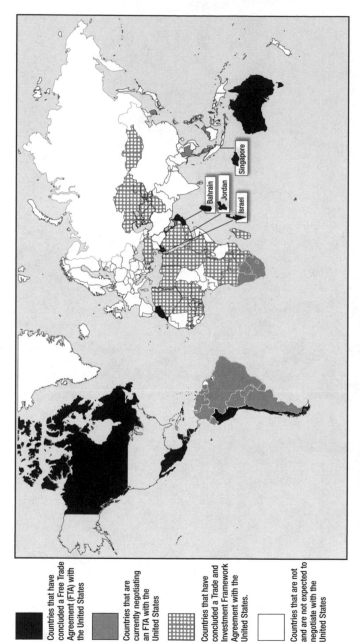

Countries that have concluded a Free Trade Agreement (FTA) with the United States

Countries that are currently negotiating an FTA with the United States

Countries that have concluded a Trade and Investment Framework Agreement with the United States.

Countries that are not and are not expected to negotiate with the United States

Source: Office of the United States Trade Representative, 2006 Trade Policy Agenda, see
http://www.ustr.gov/Document_Library/Reports_Publications/2006/2006_Trade_Policy_Agenda/Section_Index.html.

Figure 5b. Free Trade Table

COUNTRIES THAT HAVE CONCLUDED AN FTA WITH THE UNITED STATES

NAFTA 1994

Canada Mexico

CAFTA 2006

Costa Rica	Guatemala
Dominican Republic	Honduras
El Salvador	Nicaragua

Bilateral FTAs

Australia 2005	Israel 1985	Oman*
Bahrain 2006	Jordan 2001	Peru*
Chile 2004	Morocco 2004	Singapore 2004

* Awaiting ratification.

COUNTRIES CURRENTLY NEGOTIATING AN FTA WITH THE UNITED STATES

U.S.-Andean Trade Promotion Agreement 2004

Colombia Ecuador (suspended)

Sacu FTA 2003

Botswana	South Africa
Lesotho	Swaziland
Namibia	

FTAA 1994

Antigua & Barbuda	Dominica
Argentina	Dominican Republic
Bahamas	Ecuador
Barbados	El Salvador
Belize	Grenada
Bolivia	Guatemala
Brazil	Guyana
Canada	Haiti
Chile	Honduras
Colombia	Jamaica
Costa Rica	Mexico

Nicaragua	
Panama	
Paraguay	
Peru	
Saint Kitts & Nevis	
Saint Lucia	
Saint Vincent & Grenadines	
Suriname	
Trinidad & Tobago	
Uruguay	
Venezuela	

Countries Negotiating a Bilateral FTA

Malaysia 2006
Panama 2004
South Korea 2006
Thailand 2004
United Arab Emirates 2005

Dates for FTAs indicate the date they took effect; dates for negotiations indicate beginning of negotiations; current as of July 15, 2006.

U.S. Trade Strategy: Free Versus Fair

Figure 6: Status of Trade Agreements between the U.S. and Trading Partners
(as of June 13, 2006)

Country	Bilateral FTA w/ U.S.	TIFA w/ U.S.	WTO	Regional Free Trade Agreements	Other Proposed Regional Trade Agreement
Afghanistan		✓			
Albania			✓		
Algeria		✓			MEFTA
Angola		✓	✓		Common Market for Eastern and Southern Africa
Antigua & Barbuda			✓		FTAA
Argentina			✓		FTAA
Armenia			✓		
Australia	✓		✓		APEC FTA
Austria			✓		
Bahamas					FTAA
Bahrain	✓	✓	✓		
Bangladesh			✓		
Barbados			✓		FTAA
Belgium			✓		
Belize			✓		FTAA
Benin		✓	✓		West African Economic and Monetary Union
Bolivia			✓		FTAA, Andean FTA
Botswana			✓		Sacu FTA
Brazil			✓		FTAA
Brunei		✓	✓		APEC FTA
Bulgaria			✓		
Burkina Faso		✓	✓		West African Economic and Monetary Union
Burundi		✓	✓		Common Market for Eastern and Southern Africa
Cambodia			✓		
Cameroon			✓		
Canada			✓	NAFTA	FTAA, APEC FTA
Central African Republic			✓		
Chad			✓		
Chile	✓		✓		FTAA, APEC FTA
China			✓		APEC FTA
Chinese Taipei			✓		APEC FTA
Colombia			✓		FTAA, Andean FTA
Comoros		✓			Common Market for Eastern and Southern Africa
Congo			✓		
Costa Rica			✓	CAFTA	FTAA
Cote d'Ivoire		✓	✓		West African Economic and Monetary Union
Croatia			✓		
Cuba			✓		

[122]

Figure 6: Status of Trade Agreements between the U.S. and Trading Partners
(as of June 13, 2006) *(Continued)*

Country	Bilateral FTA w/ U.S.	TIFA w/ U.S.	WTO	Regional Free Trade Agreements	Other Proposed Regional Trade Agreement
Cyprus			✓		
Czech Republic			✓		
Democratic Republic of the Congo	✓		✓		Common Market for Eastern and Southern Africa
Denmark			✓		
Djibouti	✓		✓		Common Market for Eastern and Southern Africa
Dominica			✓		FTAA
Dominican Republic			✓	CAFTA	FTAA
Ecuador	Negotiations Suspended		✓		FTAA, Andean FTA
Egypt	✓		✓		MEFTA, Common Market for Eastern and Southern Africa
El Salvador			✓	CAFTA	FTAA
Eritrea	✓				Common Market for Eastern and Southern Africa
Estonia			✓		
Ethiopia	✓				Common Market for Eastern and Southern Africa
Fiji			✓		
Finland			✓		
Former Yugoslav Republic of Macedonia (FYROM)			✓		
France			✓		
Gabon			✓		
Gambia			✓		
Georgia			✓		
Germany			✓		
Ghana	✓		✓		
Greece			✓		
Grenada			✓		FTAA
Guatemala			✓	CAFTA	FTAA
Guinea Bissau	✓		✓		West African Economic and Monetary Union
Guinea			✓		
Guyana			✓		FTAA
Haiti			✓		FTAA
Honduras			✓	CAFTA	FTAA
Hong Kong			✓		APEC FTA
Hungary			✓		
Iceland			✓		
India			✓		
Indonesia			✓		APEC FTA
Iran					
Iraq					
Ireland			✓		
Israel	✓		✓		
Italy			✓		

Figure 6: Status of Trade Agreements between the U.S. and Trading Partners
(as of June 13, 2006) *(Continued)*

Country	Bilateral FTA w/ U.S.	TIFA w/ U.S.	WTO	Regional Free Trade Agreements	Other Proposed Regional Trade Agreement
Jamaica			✓		FTAA
Japan			✓		APEC FTA
Jordan	✓		✓		
Kazakhstan		✓			Central Asian Free Trade Agreement
Kenya		✓	✓		Common Market for Eastern and Southern Africa
Korea, Republic of	Negotiating		✓		APEC FTA
Kuwait		✓	✓		
Kyrgyzstan		✓	✓		Central Asian Free Trade Agreement
Latvia			✓		
Lebanon					
Lesotho			✓		Sacu FTA
Libya		✓			Common Market for Eastern and Southern Africa
Liechtenstein			✓		
Lithuania			✓		
Luxembourg			✓		
Macao			✓		
Madagascar		✓	✓		Common Market for Eastern and Southern Africa
Malawi		✓	✓		Common Market for Eastern and Southern Africa
Malaysia	Negotiating	✓	✓		APEC FTA
Maldives			✓		
Mali		✓	✓		West African Economic and Monetary Union
Malta			✓		
Mauritania			✓		
Mauritius		✓	✓		Common Market for Eastern and Southern Africa
Mexico			✓	NAFTA	FTAA, APEC FTA
Moldova			✓		
Mongolia		✓	✓		
Morocco	✓	✓	✓		
Mozambique		✓	✓		
Myanmar			✓		
Namibia			✓		Sacu FTA
Nepal			✓		
Netherlands			✓		
New Zealand			✓		APEC FTA
Nicaragua			✓	CAFTA	FTAA
Niger		✓	✓		West African Economic and Monetary Union
Nigeria		✓	✓		
Norway			✓		

Figure 6: Status of Trade Agreements between the U.S. and Trading Partners
(as of June 13, 2006) *(Continued)*

Country	Bilateral FTA w/ U.S.	TIFA w/ U.S.	WTO	Regional Free Trade Agreements	Other Proposed Regional Trade Agreement
Oman	Awaiting ratification	✓	✓		MEFTA
Pakistan			✓		
Panama	Negotiating		✓		FTAA
Papua New Guinea			✓		APEC FTA
Paraguay			✓		FTAA
Peru	Awaiting ratification		✓		FTAA, Andean FTA, APEC FTA
Philippines		✓	✓		APEC FTA
Poland			✓		
Portugal			✓		
Qatar		✓	✓		MEFTA
Romania			✓		
Russian Federation					APEC FTA
Rwanda		✓	✓		Common Market for Eastern and Southern Africa
Saint Kitts & Nevis			✓		FTAA
Saint Lucia			✓		FTAA
Saint Vincent & Grenadines			✓		FTAA
Saudi Arabia		✓	✓		MEFTA
Senegal		✓	✓		West African Economic and Monetary Union
Seychelles		✓			Common Market for Eastern and Southern Africa
Sierra Leone			✓		
Singapore	✓		✓		APEC FTA
Slovak Republic			✓		
Slovenia			✓		
Solomon Islands			✓		
South Africa		✓	✓		Sacu FTA
Spain			✓		
Sri Lanka		✓	✓		
Sudan					Common Market for Eastern and Southern Africa
Suriname			✓		FTAA
Swaziland		✓	✓		Sacu FTA, Common Market for Eastern and Southern Africa
Sweden			✓		
Switzerland			✓		
Syria		✓			
Taiwan		✓			
Tajikistan		✓			Central Asian Free Trade Agreement
Tanzania			✓		
Thailand	Negotiating	✓	✓		APEC FTA
Togo		✓	✓		West African Economic and Monetary Union
Trinidad & Tobago			✓		FTAA

Figure 6: Status of Trade Agreements between the U.S. and Trading Partners
(as of June 13, 2006) *(Continued)*

Country	Bilateral FTA w/ U.S.	TIFA w/ U.S.	WTO	Regional Free Trade Agreements	Other Proposed Regional Trade Agreement
Tunisia		✓	✓		MEFTA
Turkey		✓	✓		
Turkmenistan		✓			Central Asian Free Trade Agreement
Uganda		✓	✓		Common Market for Eastern and Southern Africa
United Arab Emirates	Negotiating	✓	✓		MEFTA
United Kingdom			✓		
Uruguay			✓		FTAA
Uzbekistan		✓			Central Asian Free Trade Agreement
Venezuela			✓		FTAA
Vietnam					APEC FTA
Yemen		✓			MEFTA
Zambia		✓	✓		Common Market for Eastern and Southern Africa
Zimbabwe		✓	✓		Common Market for Eastern and Southern Africa

Source: "2006 Trade Policy Agenda and 2005 Annual Report of the President of the United States on the Trade Agreements Programs." Available at: http://www.ustr.gov/Document_Library/Reports_Publications/2006/2006_Trade_Policy_Agenda/Section_Index.html.

Figure 7a. Top U.S. Trading Partners by Volume of Trade in Dollars*‡

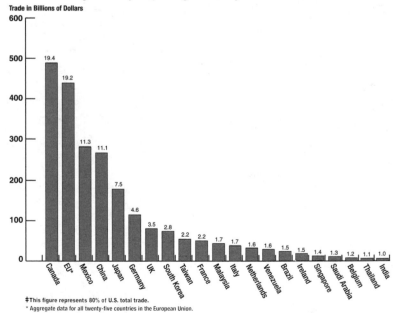

‡This figure represents 80% of U.S. total trade.
* Aggregate data for all twenty-five countries in the European Union.

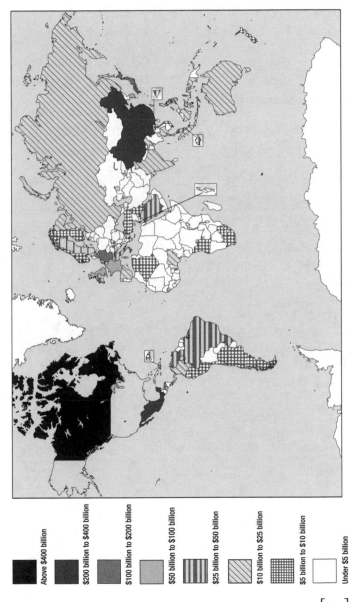

Figure 7b. Map Showing U.S. Trading Partners

Above $400 billion

$200 billion to $400 billion

$100 billion to $200 billion

$50 billion to $100 billion

$25 billion to $50 billion

$10 billion to $25 billion

$5 billion to $10 billion

Under $5 billion

CPC ADVISORY COMMITTEE

ABOUT THE AUTHOR

Daniel W. Drezner is an associate professor of international politics at the Fletcher School of Law and Diplomacy at Tufts University. He previously held teaching positions at the University of Chicago and the University of Colorado at Boulder. Drezner is the author of *The Sanctions Paradox* (Cambridge University Press, 1999) and *All Politics Is Global* (Princeton University Press, forthcoming), and the editor of *Locating the Proper Authorities* (Michigan University Press, 2003).

Professor Drezner has published articles in numerous scholarly journals as well as the *New York Times*, the *Wall Street Journal*, the *Washington Post, Foreign Affairs, Foreign Policy*, and *Slate*. He has provided expert commentary on U.S. foreign policy and the global political economy for CNNfn, CNN International, and ABC's *World News Tonight*. He has received fellowships from the German Marshall Fund of the United States, the Council on Foreign Relations, and Harvard University, and previously held positions with Civic Education Project, the RAND Corporation, and the U.S. Department of the Treasury. From 2003 to 2004, he was a monthly contributor to the New Republic Online. He keeps a daily weblog at www.danieldrezner.com.

CRITICAL POLICY CHOICES
FROM THE COUNCIL ON FOREIGN RELATIONS

Climate Change: Debating America's Policy Options (2004) by David G. Victor.

Reshaping America's Defenses: Four Alternatives (2004) by Lawrence J. Korb.

A New National Security Strategy in an Age of Terrorists, Tyrants, and Weapons of Mass Destruction (2003) by Lawrence J. Korb.

Humanitarian Intervention (2000) by Alton Frye.

Future Visions of U.S. Defense Policy (1998; revised, 2000) by John Hillen and Lawrence J. Korb.

Toward an International Criminal Court (1999) by Alton Frye.

Future Visions for U.S. Trade Policy (1998) by Bruce Stokes.

All publications listed are available on the Council on Foreign Relations website, www.cfr.org. To order printed copies, contact the Brookings Institution Press at 800-537-5487.